"Family Illustrated offers readers a humorous glimpse into the everyday happenings of J. Michael Krivyanski and his family. I'm sure it will strike a cord with those who are in the midst of parenthood. It also presents a great outlook for couples who may be on the verge of becoming first-time parents."

—Linda Auth-Gerber
Executive Editor
Professional Publications

FAMILY ILLUSTRATED

✦

AN INSTANT REPLAY OF FAMILY HUMOR

FAMILY ILLUSTRATED

◆

AN INSTANT REPLAY OF FAMILY HUMOR

J. Michael Krivyanski

iUniverse, Inc.
New York Lincoln Shanghai

FAMILY ILLUSTRATED
AN INSTANT REPLAY OF FAMILY HUMOR

iUniverse books may be ordered through booksellers or by contacting:

iUniverse
2021 Pine Lake Road, Suite 100
Lincoln, NE 68512
www.iuniverse.com
1-800-Authors (1-800-288-4677)

ISBN: 0-595-33580-2

Printed in the United States of America

This book is dedicated to my lovely wife Leatrice and wonderful daughter Alexandra. They have both provided many great ideas to write about in my humor columns by just being themselves. I thank my wife and daughter for giving me all the love and support any humor writing guy could desire.

Contents

INTRODUCTION xi

IN THE BEGINNING 1

NEW DEVELOPMENTS 4

SPECIAL DELIVERY 7

NEW HOME RULER 10

FIRST TIME FATHERHOOD 13

DATING DAUGHTER 16

PRESCHOOL PROFESSOR 19

LIKE DAUGHTER, LIKE FATHER 22

THE JOYS OF FATHERHOOD 25

PROTECTIVE PARENTING 28

B-DAY 31

FIRST GRADE FOLLIES 34

TRANSFORMATION TO GRANDPARENT 37

FOOD FIGHTING 40

COMMUNICATION CODE 43

YE OLE YARD SALE 46

AGELESS UNDERSTANDING 49

TAX GIRL 52

MYSTERY GROWING 55

GOTTA' DANCE 57

PARENTAL GROWING PAINS 60

A LESSON FOR DAD 63

TO TELL THE TRUTH 65

VACATION ANARCHY 67

CAFETERIA WOES 70

PET PEEVES 73

HORSE SENSE 76

POLITICAL COMPROMISE 79

UNTECHNO DAD 82

UNRECOGNIZABLE 84

A COMMITMENT IS A COMMITMENT 87

INTRODUCTION

This book is for all the unknown superheroes of our world. People who are all around us and commonly referred to as dedicated and loving parents.

It's not easy being such a superhero. They're able to comfort a crying child who fell as they dig through garbage in search of a dental retainer and smile during the entire experience. They pack lunches while mostly asleep and provide such surprises as a package of yeast or dried beans for their child's noontime meal. They're chauffeurs, cooks, crisis counselors, home repair contractors, toy repair people, home decorators, medics and so many other things it's impossible to list them all.

They never get media attention about all the time they spend caring for their children. They don't get recognition for keeping their children out of trouble and teaching them right from wrong. It never registers with anyone how they push themselves when they're exhausted, handle themselves when they're worried or keep their emotions under control when they know their children have to learn a difficult lesson in life.

Parents do this because that's the job of a parent. They're motivated by love and a desire to see their children happy. They don't view their sacrifices as anything beyond the ordinary. Their rewards are watching their child get that diploma, walk down the isle or be happy with their job. The biggest reward for loving and dedicated parents is when their own children grow and become parents that are just as loving and dedicated.

Many people view a superhero as someone that does the extraordinary and thinks of it as ordinary. I think that is a perfect description for all the loving and dedicated parents of our world.

IN THE BEGINNING

When I got married I was very content with the way things were in my life. My wife and I had nice jobs, we were able to go places, buy things we wanted and had what many would consider pretty fulfilling lives. It wasn't the perfect Shangri-La but for me it felt pretty close.

For some unknown reason my wife started to change after a few years. She began looking at children in a completely different way. She would stop and stare at women with babies. Babysitting a friend's child had become one of her favorite activities. I often found her in a children's clothing store smiling and holding up clothes and informing the world around her that this particular item met her standard of cute. As a thickheaded male I had no idea what was happening to her. She would try and give me subtle hints that would always go right over my head.

"Why are you always looking at baby stuff?"

"Oh, I don't know."

"Your sister's baby is having its first birthday soon isn't it?"

After a dramatic sigh she would hold up the baby clothes and look at me in a rather peculiar way.

"I think she's lucky to have a baby, don't you?"

"Actually I think her husband is lucky to have that big screen television of theirs. I sure hope we can afford one soon. I'd love to watch the play-off games on one of those."

My wife became upset, quickly put down the baby clothes and pushed me out of the way. She walked out of the store muttering something about men not being able to figure out anything. She was frustrated because I didn't get her subtle hints. At the time I thought she was angry because we had to wait to buy a big screen television.

Over a period of time my wife's mood became a little murky. I figured it had something to do with one of our sports teams losing so close in a big play-off game. I felt I understood what she was experiencing. Sports can do that to us die-hard fans and it takes time to get over the disappointment.

1

It happened one day that my lovely wife summoned up her nerve and confronted me with what was on her mind. It was a challenge for her to get me to understand what she was saying.

"Mike, we both agreed before we got married that we wanted to have a family some day. I want to have a baby."

"You want to baby-sit someone else's child again today?"

"No, I've been thinking and I feel the time is right for us to have a baby of our very own."

"Baby what? We can't have pets in this apartment. It was in the lease we signed."

My wife sat down beside me and slowly put her arm on my shoulder. She spoke in a soft and gentle voice.

"Don't be silly. I want to get pregnant and have a child, our child."

It was as if a bolt of lightening hit me. I was stunned. My throat went dry and I began to take deep breaths as I chattered like an idiot.

"Yeah, well, ah, hey, I mean, you know, ah, a baby, that's sure something, wow, I mean a baby, hey that's, sure is a, yeah, we, ah, is the game on?"

My wife held my hand and continued looking into my eyes.

"I love you and I know you love me and what could be more natural than for a married couple in love to have a baby together?"

I began to sweat and tried to swallow. She was serious, very serious. For some reason I was nervous, very nervous. This is when our different views on having a child became apparent. We began to play dueling reasoning.

"Think of all the expense," I muttered.

"Think of being able to experience the miracle of birth," she replied.

"I experienced that when I was born and I don't remember a thing. Think of all the diapers, food, clothes, a crib, high chair, play pen and bottles. That stuff is really expensive."

"Think of coming home and being called Mommy and Daddy."

"We're talking a lot of money here. Think of all the doctor's visits, braces, college tuition not to mention eye doctors and maybe even glasses."

"Seeing your child grow and change. School projects, reading to them and lots of hugs and kisses."

"Taking on a second job and maybe a third. I may not see the child until it's old enough to retire."

As if my wife had become possessed by my very own mother she stood up and put her hands on her hips. She then began using my full name while lecturing me.

"What makes you think if we have a child life won't be better than it is right now? You need to stop feeling like this is the worst thing you could experience and understand it's the most wonderful thing two people could ever do with their lives."

Anyone who had been lectured by a spouse knows it's a total recall of feelings from childhood. I almost headed to my room. When I realized my fear was based on not having faith in myself and confidence in our marriage I began to see things in a different way. With the fear gone the idea of having a child was pretty neat. With a child around people wouldn't look at me so strange when I tested the toys at the toy store. If it was a boy I could teach him about sports. If it was a girl I could teach her about sports. When I thought about it again I felt warm inside and happy. I stood up, hugged my wife and told her she was right. I would try to be a good father. She would do the same at being a mother.

"I love you, hon."

"I love you too, so much."

We held each other and both knew we were at the beginning of a very special journey together.

NEW DEVELOPMENTS

Men who think their wives are a little on the cranky side of things once a month have never experienced anything like a pregnant woman. Many men fail to grasp the concept that these ladies are experiencing some rather serious hormonal explosions. Their female bodies are entering a period of constant transformation unlike anything the male mind can comprehend. A pregnant woman's body is slowly turning into a biological manufacturing complex. Since the product has to be finished in nine months the complex is kicked into high gear and is on autopilot. During the process women will have a mobile baby-traveling center built within them. It will come complete with Mom's down home umbilical cord food source and a rather comfortable pool-type environment.

The only problem is that men have no ability to relate in any way to what their wives are experiencing. A man's body is a rather simple mechanism created to mow the lawn, watch television and play softball. At least that's what me and many of my friends have concluded.

Pregnancy is a time when your wife is riding an emotional roller coaster. The most trivial, insignificant things can take on major importance.

"How could you?"

"What?"

"You put spoons in the fork spot in the silverware drawer."

"Yeah. So, what's the big deal?"

"Men, you're all the same. Think you can go and get your wife pregnant then do anything you want with the silverware drawer."

This is the time when the well-prepared man will run to the freezer in their refrigerator. Inside he will have a container of his wife's favorite ice cream marked "For Emergencies Only." He will then quickly put a spoonful of the ice cream in his wife's mouth while she's yelling at him.

"You're all despicable creatures you men, you, mmmmmmmmmmmm that's pretty good. Hey, I like that a lot. What was I saying?"

"Nothing, dear."

Emergency ice cream is a survival technique for a husband with a pregnant wife that is only discussed during breaks at sporting events.

To help with the experience of having a child our society has created classes on baby delivery. This is a place where new couples learn how the wife will be in gut-wrenching agony during the baby's birth. The role of the useless husband is to attempt to get his wife's mind off of the pain by holding her hand, breathing and counting. After this lesson men become glad they're men and women plan revenge.

To back up their claims of childbirth these places show movies to the expect-ant couples. Not your first-run Hollywood-type movies but the kind of movies that actually show women delivering babies. This was a flashback for me to my health class in high school. I was able to avoid any type of uncomfortable health movie by getting the hall pass and staying in the bathroom until class was over. When the birthing class would show these women having babies type movies I would just go to the bathroom and stay there until the end of class. I was a rather shy guy and felt the old movies showing fathers pacing up and down in the wait-ing room while smoking cigars was my type of baby delivery movie. Until the birthing class was willing to show those kind of movies the bathroom was the place for me.

After the first class my wife caught onto me and I was in trouble.

"Where you going?"

"To the bathroom."

"Oh, no you don't. Last time you stayed in there until the birthing class was over. You're not going to do that again."

"But I have a hall pass."

"Too bad."

"Have they started showing movies on men pacing in waiting rooms and smoking cigars?"

"You'll be with me when the baby arrives, remember?"

"Why would you want to deliver the baby in a waiting room with pacing guys smoking cigars?"

"Sit down."

During the class we learned the biological aspects of what was going to occur on the day of the baby's arrival. We learned about procedures that could happen at the hospital. The men practiced holding the hand of their wife while helping them breathe and count. At the end we felt ready. My wife was anxious to get the delivery over with and I couldn't wait to walk around in a hospital wearing real hospital scrubs.

The last few months of the pregnancy are the most interesting. People can put their hands on the mother's stomach and feel the baby kick and move. Sometimes interesting womb conversations are made with the unborn child.

"Hey you, yeah you inside the womb. I'm going to have your Mom send down some of this new cereal and if you like it, kick on the sides and I'll make sure we have plenty for when you get here."

Sometimes my wife would just look at me and shake her head. She had no appreciation for the many thought provoking womb conversations I had with our yet to be born child.

I've read about miracles but never thought I'd ever experience one. That all changed when I would look at my wife during the pregnancy. I realized it was a real human being and our very own child who was developing inside her.

SPECIAL DELIVERY

I must have watched way too much television when I was growing up. This was evident the day my daughter made her way into the world. I handled this situation by acting like an expectant father in a television sitcom. To the observer it was funny but to the participants it had little or no humor.

The blessed event started to occur on a rather typical day when my lovely wife just looked at me and started yelling about these things that she was experiencing called contractions.

"The contractions are coming closer together and I think you should call the doctor."

Panic set in and I began to put my natural ability to be an idiot into action.

"Yes, I'll call the doctor. What will I call him? I mean what will I tell him?"

My wife waddled over to me, grabbed me by my ear and yelled "Look, Bub, the baby is about to be born and the doctor needs to know, AAAAAAAGH."

So I called the doctor. The doctor asked if my wife was in extreme discomfort. Discomfort is a hospital buzzword for pain and extreme discomfort is a hospital buzzword for gut-wrenching agony.

I looked over at my wife who was doubled over and groaning. I remained calm and relayed to my wife the questions the doctor was asking me.

"Hon, the doctor would like to know if you are experiencing any discomfort?"

With an ear-shattering scream my wife yelled, "I'm having the worst pain I've ever experienced in my life you bonehead."

"Doctor, I can honestly say my wife has sincerely expressed that the pain level she is experiencing at the moment could easily be classified as extreme discomfort. I think we might want to bring her to the hospital."

For some reason on the way to the hospital my wife was not her usual talkative self. I began to realize that the big moment was upon us. My wife would be able to deliver our baby and I would be able to wear real hospital scrubs. We were both excited.

What I found most interesting when we got to the hospital was the number of people who visited the delivery room to check on my wife. It seemed like all hospital personal within a ten-mile radius were there to be a part of what was happening.

I saw so many people in there it was like she was delivering the baby in a sports arena. I'm not sure but I think I saw a hospital orderly selling tickets outside her delivery room.

"See yer' baby delivery here. See it while it actually happens. Live before your very eyes. Great seats still available."

"Where you think yer' going buddy?"

"I'm the father."

"You get a discount but I can't guarantee a good seat."

"Thanks."

While people were checking on my wife I put on my hospital scrubs. I soon learned there is actually a back and front to those things and the foot things don't fit on your head. It was a valuable learning experience.

During the delivery I forgot how to count or breathe like we were taught in our birthing class. To make up for this I babbled senselessly and that seemed to entertain my wife and the nurses. Luckily my wife remembered what I was supposed to do and in a short time we were back on track. It's a good thing she was with me. I'm sure I couldn't have done it without her.

These contraction things kept coming closer and closer together according to my wife. For some reason this put her in a rather bad mood and after a series of very strong ones she said some rather unflattering things about me, my parents, my grandparents and our family pet. I was also informed with some very strong language that my sex life was over for eternity and I put my life on the line if she ever caught me even thinking about it.

My wife was doing her best and I was very nervous about things. The nurses and doctors seemed extremely calm. They talked about important matters such as their favorite house decorations and new ways to improve the look of their lawns. I took this as a sign there were no problems with the delivery or these people were planning to leave the medical profession to pursue careers in interior designing and landscaping.

All of a sudden the doctor pulled out a baby's head. In one quick moment I was a father. I looked at my daughter for the first time. My new daughter looked at me and started to cry. I started to cry. The baby was placed on my wife's chest and my wife started to cry.

I looked at my wife and we began to spout gibberish at each other.

"Ag, da, she, beautiful baby, oh, man, I love you."

"She, a, yeah, baby, ours, oh, its, ah, I love you too."

The first thing they did was put my daughter on a newborn baby tanning bed. I guess they didn't want her to be self-conscious with other tanned babies when we took her to the beach. Then they took her down to where the other newborn babies were and put her behind what looked like a department store display window. Behind the big glass partition parents, relatives and friends would point to the babies and make strange faces, weird sounds and act like it was improv' night at the hospital.

As I stood among them looking at my new daughter I was very happy. During my life I'd always been thankful for the many gifts I'd experienced but I had never experienced anything this wonderful. The world now looked new to me. I realized our child had just begun the process of changing me into a better person than I ever thought possible.

NEW HOME RULER

There was a time before we brought my newborn baby daughter home from the hospital that I thought of myself as a "take charge" kind of guy. I was very confident in my ability to handle any situation that came my way. With the birth of our daughter that perception of myself was changed forever.

Upon arrival to our home this little person took complete and total control of every aspect of our lives. Like a powerful little dictator she absolutely refused to consider the possibility of ever relinquishing her power.

As a new father I had so much to learn. My first lesson was that this tiny creature who weighed less than ten pounds was now the new sheriff in town. Armed with just a healthy set of lungs and a highly functional voice box this little person set about turning me and my wife into her personal servants. We became totally dedicated to taking care of her every need and desire.

"Waaaaaaaaaaaaaaaaaaaaaaaaa."

"Sweetheart, daddy is watching a very important game. Please stop crying. I'll get you your bottle right after this play."

"WAAAAAAAAAAAAAAAAAAAAAAAAAAAAAAAAAA."

"All right, all right, I'm sorry. I don't know what I was thinking."

When I was a kid one of the biggest challenges for us boys was to think of new and innovative methods to gross each other out. We'd do this in various creative ways and especially when armed with cafeteria food. If you could get someone to hold their mouth while running from the cafeteria it was a good day.

I've come to realize we were nothing but a bunch of low ranking gross-out amateurs. The experience of changing the diaper of a newborn baby is probably on display at the gross-out hall of fame.

"AAAAH, whoa, hey, this kid wins the gross-out contest and is the official champion. She is impressive because she didn't even need cafeteria food to do it."

"What are you talking about?"

"Never mind."

The little new boss also attracted more attention than a movie star. After we brought my daughter home from the hospital we were besieged by people with cameras, video recorders and every other photographic recording device known.

This was an effort by friends and family to try and get any type photographic image of the new baby for themselves.

"Hey who are you guys?"

"We're the parents."

"Could you move out of the way? We're trying to get a picture of the baby."

I must admit that my wife and I gave into the urge to photographically record every detail of our new daughter's existence. We were quickly turning into your basic "Paparazzi" and "Mamarazzi."

"Look, she yawned. Did you get a picture?'

"Yeah and from a new angle too. That gives us 47 yawning pictures."

"Great, those will go well with the 39 sleeping pictures. I'm sure she'll love to look at these when she gets older."

We were very proud parents. At work my office was transformed from a place of business to a living memorial of my family. Pictures of my wife and daughter covered almost every space on the wall and desk of my office. I thought about charging admission but decided my boss might not agree to it even if I gave him a good discount.

People began avoiding me at work because I viewed every conversation as an opportunity to talk about my new baby daughter.

"Did you get that report done?"

"Yes I did but wait until you hear what my daughter did while I was working on the report."

"If you talk about your daughter one more time I just might scream."

"That's good to know. She was so cute when my wife fed her last night."

I guess I didn't really know when to stop.

One fact I observed about relatives is they like to discuss a child's physical features and assign responsibility to certain people in the family. This would be fine but then arguments seem to always follow.

"Look, she's got her mom's eyes."

"No she doesn't. Her eyes are brown like her dad's."

"Look, she's got her dad's nose."

"Anybody can see that's the mom's nose."

"Be glad she doesn't have your nose."

"Oh yeah and why is that?"

"Because it's going to be broken pretty soon."

One of the most interesting aspects of having a child is trying to guess what they will become when they get older. My wife felt our daughter obviously would be an artist by the way she would get excited every time she would look at a painting shown to her. I told my wife she was laughing because of the funny faces my wife made while showing our daughter the pictures. I said our daughter was going to become a sports announcer because of the faces she made whenever I turned on a sports game. My wife disagreed with me and felt it was because our daughter had gas.

Maybe it's good that parents don't know the future of their children because we have no real control over it anyway. All we can do as parents is love our children, be there for them when they need us and hope for the best. Just the way most families have done for generations of children.

FIRST TIME FATHERHOOD

After my daughter was born I quickly discovered that being a first-time father could actually be considered a scary experience. It's not on the scale of being forced to face down a charging Grizzly bear with a bag of marshmallows or your in laws coming to stay with no planned departure date but it's up there on the scary scale.

Since I was the youngest in my family I had no experience with babies. When I was growing up babies were very little people that smelled funny and were quickly given back to relatives whenever they started to cry. Dealing with babies didn't seem like a difficult thing back then.

When my lovely wife was pregnant I had dreams of how my family would look. In our home I would be holding my child with my wife by my side. We would laugh and have fun in the ultimate family experience. The three of us would be a Norman Rockwell painting and a Hallmark greeting card all rolled into one.

When my daughter arrived I soon realized that greeting cards and paintings don't depict the harsh reality of parenthood.

Maybe not too many greeting cards would get sold if they pictured a parent with bloodshot eyes putting a diaper on their child's stuffed animal in the middle of the night. Would the greeting card then show the bare bottomed child smiling at their parents while relieving themselves all over the crib? Is it possible that nobody would want to see the painting of a parent frantically rocking their crying baby while singing made-up words off key in a desperate attempt to get their child to sleep?

The one thing I noticed when we brought my daughter home from the hospital is that the daily activities of babies are very limited. They cry, they eat, they relieve themselves and they sleep. I never realized how much time these activities could take until we had a child. My daughter's daily itinerary did not have much variety but her schedule kept us quite busy.

I quickly realized that babies are sometimes like miniature extortionists. They refuse to negotiate and will constantly demand clean diapers and formula from their parents by any means available to them. I tried to talk to my daughter and see if I could explain the virtues of not crying so much at night. I made her an offer I thought was more than fair.

"Sweetheart, if you can let Mommy and Daddy get some rest tonight I'll buy you a sports car for your sixteenth birthday."

In a true gesture of father-daughter bonding my wonderful child looked up at me, burped and went to sleep. I was happy she was asleep and impressed by the loudness of her burp.

My wife and I both changed with the arrival of our daughter. For her part my wife developed an advanced radar detection system. It enabled her to know when my daughter needed to be changed or fed at anytime during the day or night. She was able to decipher the meaning of our daughter's crying.

In the middle of the night my daughter would start to cry and my wife would say, "She's hungry and needs to be changed."

When I asked how she knew this I was certain my wife would give me a very detailed and scientific explanation.

She simply looked at me, shrugged her shoulders and said, "Because I do."

For my part I discovered that I possessed a rather impressive ability to make silly faces that made my daughter laugh. I had no idea how good at silly-face-making I was until I started doing this for my daughter at a park. People around me started laughing and clapping. I never thought having a child would enable me to discover such an impressive hidden talent.

One of the scariest moments of becoming a father was when all the things my own parents told me while growing up started to make sense. I began to feel their emotions and know their fears. It was like experiencing a revelation.

There was a time when my newborn daughter was fussing and on impulse I stepped back and said "You keep up with this and you can forget about going out tonight with your friends."

I started looking around the room for my parents. It was almost as if I was possessed.

In a short time things changed with my daughter. The first time she slept through the night my wife and I both woke up at the same time and ran into her room feeling terrified and thinking something terrible had happened. We found her asleep in her crib, the picture of a babe in dreamland. Soon our fears began to give way as my wife and I realized that we were actually good parents. We were doing the right things with raising our child. This feeling gave us confidence to face the next set of challenges that always come when raising children.

In a matter of time our daughter no longer needed diapers and moved on to other developmental stages. It happened so quickly. I have this image in my mind of my wife and I holding a rattle for our daughter but turning around to see her drive off to college. I've had other parents tell me time passed so quickly with their children that's what it felt like for them.

I was looking at a picture of the three of us the other day.

I showed it to my wife and said, "Don't we look just like a Norman Rockwell painting?"

She smiled and said, "No, I think we look more like a Hallmark greeting card."

Who says dreams don't come true?

DATING DAUGHTER

A friend of mine said something to me the other day that was so upsetting I felt that taking drastic measures were in order. I have considered removing him from my holiday card list and intend to ignore his very existence at social gatherings.

This unforgivable incident occurred when we were sitting at his house having a friendly father-to-father type conversation. He started telling me about his two teenage daughters and their dating behaviors. These young ladies of his would both come home late from dates with some very creative excuses that consisted of everything from "I forgot what time it was" to the witty and timeless classic "We got lost."

I started laughing as he told me these stories. That was when my friend made the most reprehensible, mean-spirited and vengeful statement one father could ever say to another. He told me not to laugh at him because in time my little daughter would grow up and turn into a teenager just like his daughters had done. Then I'd have all the pleasure of dealing with the things he was dealing with right now.

How low can you get?

I assured him I would approach this dating stuff in a whole different way. My daughter would not be allowed to date until she reached the reasonable age of about forty-seven. Then only if she has her blackbelt in karate, kung fu and has won a few matches in professional wrestling. The guy who might be considered for taking my daughter out on a date would have to pass a background check by the FBI, CIA, IRS and the US Postal Service. I'm not taking any chances.

My friend then sat back with a smug smile and started laughing and shaking his head.

He then looked at me and said, "Just wait. You just wait and see what happens."

When I told my wife about this incident she provided me with some insight into her own dark and murky past. She confessed to me that she herself had once been a teenage girl and had actually gone on dates with boys. I just wish she had told me about this bizarre and twisted behavior before we got married. I had no idea I'd married a woman with a past.

My wife called this teenage dating stuff "normal" and "a part of growing up." She told me things like girls need to learn how to go on dates and I was over reacting. Where she came up with these very distorted views is beyond me.

She looked at me and asked if I ever thought about how the fathers felt when I was a teenager and would take their daughters out on dates. I thought about it for a minute.

"Another man's problem," I yelled.

I began to tell my wife about my dating daughter strategy. I told her that since our daughter is so young I've got plenty of time to make plans.

"By the time our daughter gets ready to date I can have our entire house prepared. I'm going to dig a fifty-foot hole and disguise it as our walkway. That'll make them boys think twice before they try to take my daughter on a date."

"Mike, you're being ridiculous" my wife pleaded.

"If they get past that I'm going to have a moat under our doorstep filled with teenage boy eating piranhas."

"Mike, will you stop it."

"The best one of all is how I'm going to place a nest of killer bees just inside the doorway so it will fall on them right before they get into the house. That'll give those date-wanting boys a whole new attitude."

"Mike, you're being an idiot."

"I guess you probably think the machine gun nest I want to build on the roof is a bad idea?"

That's when my wife put her hands on her hips and gave me "the look." Any man who has been married for any length of time knows what it's like when his wife gives him "the look." It's an expression that says your wife is right, you are wrong and it's about time you accept that fact. Advancing armies around the world could be stopped dead in their tracks if they just had their wives stand in front of them giving "the look."

I suppose I get a little crazy when it comes to my daughter. She's not just another child. This is the little girl I watched being born. I've changed her diapers, given her baths and gotten baby barf stains on my clothes from her. I've sung songs to her until my throat was reduced to a whisper so she would go to sleep. I've been up all night with her when she was sick and cleaned up the mess. I've gotten her snacks, watched videos and played games like Candyland with her until I felt a part of some board game playing endurance test. She's so special to me.

Many parents have told me that letting go is never easy but a fact of life that must happen.

I know when the time comes I will find a way to gracefully accept the many changes that will turn my little daughter into a grown woman. I'll probably be just like so many other fathers who have daughters. It will never matter to me how big my daughter gets because in my heart she'll always be that little girl I made funny faces for in the park on a warm spring day.

PRESCHOOL PROFESSOR

I've always thought of myself as a fairly knowledgeable guy. When it comes to education I did well enough in college to earn a degree. When it comes to traveling I've seen everything from the pyramids in Egypt to the Vatican City. When it comes to experiences I've served in the military and even worked for a private detective. I also do a pretty good job at answering the questions on Jeopardy.

I just wish someone would explain why my little daughter is always enlightening me about some aspect of life that I was previously unaware existed. Maybe I'm just naive of the many things our daughter is knowledgeable about in the world.

A bath to me has always been an activity where you washed yourself. My daughter has been nice enough to provide us with some new and different insights on the activity of bathing.

"Dad, I wanna' play with that toy."

"Sweetheart it's not a toy, it's just a bar of soap."

"No it's not. It's a slippery fish."

The bar of soap is then squeezed through her hands several times. She smiles as it drops into the water and sinks to the bottom.

"Dad, I wanna' play with that toy."

"Sweetheart it's just a wash cloth."

"No it's not. It's a snake."

She takes the end of the wash cloth and guides it through the water while saying "Aaaah, snake."

I'm then told the story of how the slippery fish and the snake become friends and help each other out in the ocean where they live. I must have missed that one when it was in the news. It would be difficult to describe my feelings of embarrassment for not being able to properly recognize these common bath items as actual characters in a popular bath time play.

Eating a meal has turned out to be another educational experience for me. Since the arrival of our daughter we no longer dine on spaghetti like other people. We eat wild snake noodles with sauce. The proper way to refer to rice that has butter mixed with it is rice that looks like popcorn. I've also been made aware that to eat cereal with any spoon other than the special color-changing one you got from another box of cereal is to commit a serious breach of kid breakfast eating etiquette.

My child has also taken it upon herself to inform me about some of the more frightening aspects of life. It seems that at nighttime she is the only one in our house who comes face-to-face with monsters that live in her room.

The other night I was awakened out of a very peaceful sleep by my daughter who informed me there were monsters in her room. I handled the situation like any mature and rational adult. I marched into her bedroom and sprayed them with imaginary anti-monster spray. Five minutes later I was awakened and informed that the monsters were gone but now giant spiders were in her room. I asked my daughter what we should do to make them leave. She then explained that sleeping with her parents would make them all go away. Since we were all out of imaginary anti-spider spray I agreed.

Before becoming a parent I heard a nasty rumor about kids and boxes that turned out to be very true. Children do prefer boxes to the toys that came in them. I bought my daughter an expensive toy and anticipated that she would be filled with so much joy upon seeing it that people from the Fatherhood Hall of Fame would rush to our house and instantly induct me as an honorary member.

After a few hours of watching this toy do nothing while the box got all the attention I tried to understand my daughter.

"Why are you playing in the box?"

"Because I want to."

"Why aren't you playing with the nice toy Daddy got you?"

"Because I don't want to."

"Does it matter that the toy is worth a year of college tuition?"

"No."

With that type of honesty I realized she had no future in politics.

At times my daughter has a special way of putting life in its proper perspective. Recently, I had a bill returned to me because I forgot to put a stamp on the envelope. I sat there thinking about all the additional charges I would have to pay and I felt embarrassed. My daughter saw me and reacted.

"Why are you so sad, Daddy?"

"Oh, because sometimes your daddy does stupid things."

She quickly crawled into my lap and gave me a hug.

"You're not stupid, Daddy. You're beautiful and I love you."

All the love and acceptance I saw in her eyes would be difficult to describe.

Becoming a father has enabled me to recall a period in my life that seems so long ago. A time when the story of Santa Claus made perfect sense and my entire world centered around watching cartoons and playing with G.I. Joe. A time that seems lost forever.

As a dad I've learned it doesn't seem to matter how much I may know about being a parent, because it's my daughter who still has a lot to teach me about being a kid.

LIKE DAUGHTER, LIKE FATHER

As a parent I'm always watching my daughter's behavior change as she gets older. I've noticed that some rather interesting things occur when my daughter has to do something that does not appeal to her. This is a time when she transforms from a brilliant young girl into someone who seems to have mold for brain cells. I call this behavior the "Huh? What? Syndrome."

After speaking to a number of parents I've come to realize that this syndrome runs rampant among many school-aged children. Some parents have told me this syndrome has actually plagued generations of children in some families.

It all starts when I try to get my daughter to do something that has gotten a low rating on the child fun scale. If I tell her to go play on the computer, watch TV or eat her favorite snack she'll leave so fast all you'll see is a cloud of dust like she's a character in a Warner Brothers cartoon. Take this exact same child who understands every connotation and denotation of the words computer game, potato chips or television and tell her it's time to change clothes and get ready for school. The symptoms of this syndrome suddenly begin to appear at an alarming rate.

This otherwise brilliant child now transforms into someone who has no idea what I'm talking about or even who I am. This is the exact moment when I realize the "Huh? What? Syndrome" has taken a firm grip on my child.

"Sweetheart it's time to go change your clothes and get ready for school."

"Huh?"

"I said go change your clothes."

"What?"

"Go change your clothes."

"Who are you? And why can't I finish watching my favorite TV program?"

"Hey, I'm your dad and it's almost time to leave for school."

"I don't want to do whatever it was you just talked about."

"It's almost time for school. Now get in your room and change those clothes."

When I turn off the television my daughter looks at me as if I just told her it was actually Big Bird we ate last night for dinner. After a rather dramatic sigh she slowly meanders toward her bedroom dragging a one-eyed teddy bear. Anyone just coming upon this scene would think she'd just been sentenced to work on a kindergarten chain gang.

Once inside her bedroom the syndrome continues. My daughter looks around her room and knows she is supposed to be doing something. Her mind starts contemplating a series of complex questions in an effort to unfold the deep mystery of why she is now in her bedroom.

"Did it involve a snack? That couldn't be it. Could it involve the computer? No, the computers' not in my bedroom. I think I'm supposed to change the clothes on something. I bet it's one of my Barbie dolls. Yeah, that's got to be it."

She then begins to play with her Barbie dolls, totally oblivious to any conversation that has recently transpired between the two of us.

A few minutes later I go to see what's going on in her room.

"Are you dressed yet?"

"No."

"Why not?"

"I forgot."

For all of you expectant first time parents "I forgot" is a phrase of almost as much importance to a young child as "free candy." It's a catchall phrase that can be skillfully employed in any situation where the child is trying to avoid some type of punishment.

At this point I'm a little aggravated so I let her know.

"If you don't get changed in five minutes you won't get any television and no time on the computer until you're old enough to vote."

Now the symptoms of the "Huh, What Syndrome" slowly begin to disappear. With the prospects of no television and no time on the computer my daughter's mind moves with amazing precision. She gets dressed so quickly I think I should call Ripley's Believe It or Not.

When my wife returns home I decide to find out what she thinks about our child's behavior.

"Did you ever see anybody act like that before?"

"Yeah I have seen someone act like that many times. You act just like our daughter all the time."

"What are you talking about?"

"If I ask you to go shopping with me you always act like I'm taking you to visit some kind of a torture chamber."

"Yeah, well, you know, it is shopping stuff."

"But if I tell you one of your sports programs is on you run for the television like some professional football player heading for the end zone."

"Well I suppose it could be interpreted that way."

"Whenever it comes to doing something you don't like it always seems like you develop selective amnesia. Did you take out the garbage like I asked you?"

"Well, not really. I actually kind of forgot."

"Do you see what I mean?"

After a dramatic sigh my wife departs the room shaking her head and muttering something about being married to Peter Pan.

It's painfully obvious my wife is right but I wisely resisted the temptation to give her a raspberry.

I suppose one of the most interesting things you experience after becoming a parent is realizing the more you look at your kids, the more you can see yourself.

THE JOYS OF FATHERHOOD

My wife has a unique way of getting me to correct some of my bad behaviors. She does this when I don't know my behaviors are bad or that she is in the process of correcting them. Her tactic is to let me hang myself by manipulating my inbred, natural, stereotypical male-ego-driven responses to certain situations. If she feels I'm not spending enough time with our daughter she doesn't say anything to me but will simply go away for the weekend.

"I'm going to visit my sister for the weekend. Do you think you could handle things here while I'm gone or do I need to call a baby and daddy sitter?"

I quickly dropped the newspaper I was reading, stood up and began to lecture my wife about the facts of the man she had married.

"Handle things? Madam do you realize just whom it is you are talking with at the moment? I happen to be an educated, competent man who has impressed people with his creativity and resourcefulness. What possible reason would you have to doubt my abilities in caring for our child by myself?"

"Last time you watched my sister's children they didn't have a bath for two days, there was mold on the dishes when I came home and the only edible thing in the house was crumbs from fast food bags."

"Yeah, but we survived."

"I'll leave my sister's number next to the phone so it doesn't have to be looked up."

"You don't have to worry about a thing because we'll be just fine."

"Her number isn't for you, it's for our daughter. She may need to be talked through bath procedures."

On the first day of my wife's absence our daughter came into the living room and said she was hungry. I realized that children are not just fun to be with but also need to be fed.

"What would you like to eat sweetheart?"

"I don't know."

"What do you want to have?"

"Something."

"Like what?"

"I don't know."

I decided to suggest a universal favorite among kids.

"How about a hamburger?"

"Yes."

I discovered getting my daughter to decide what to eat was easier than preparing it for her.

"What would you like on it?"

"The regular stuff."

"What is the regular stuff?"

"Mom knows."

Reluctantly I called my wife. It would have probably been easier to design a space station than to fix my daughter's lunch.

My culinary skills were greatly enhanced as I learned how to have just the right proportions of catsup, mustard and a *smidgen* of mayonnaise. I asked my wife to define smidgen and she couldn't but she knew what it was so I winged it. I had to use regular bread and the crusts had to be cut off, the hamburger had to be cut in half and the pickle, hamburger and potato chips had to be arranged in the shape of a face on her plate.

"What happens if it's not given to her in the shape of a face?"

"You don't want to know."

She then told me the many details about our daughter's dinner and breakfast meals. I began to think our daughter should come with a meal time instruction manual.

Later that night I informed my daughter it was time for bath. She got in the bathroom looked at me and put her hands on her hips.

"Where's my toys?"

"Look, you're here to wash and get out. What toys could you possibly need?"

"Mom knows."

We experienced bath stoppage for lack of appropriate toys as I scoured our house with the intensity of a search for buried treasure. I was once again forced to call my wife. This time she wasn't at all polite about inappropriate laughter.

"What do you mean the sponge animals, bath paints and deep blue sea doll are in the bathroom closet, inside a plastic container marked bath toys? You talk like everyone would've looked there first or something."

After bath my daughter informed me it was time for snack, then her sing-along video. With my wife gone this meant I had to do more at bedtime than quit watching television and start reading the newspaper.

There are many unwritten video-watching and snack-eating rules that I unknowingly stumbled upon. Snack is a point to ponder as choices are read to the child. After Dad displays sufficient frustration a choice is made and snack is gotten. Snack has to be there before the video starts. If snack is not there before video starts child's whining mechanism is triggered and is only disengaged when Dad begins yelling that videos and snacks are not necessary to sustain life on this planet.

The next day was very special to me as my daughter opened up her five-year-old world. I learned about the playground at school and the value of having special rocks. She told me about games she plays with her friends and the names of all her favorite stuffed animals. I was even taken outside in our yard and shown her "special" place. The sky, bugs, plants, animals of any kind were a new and fascinating experience she wanted to share with me. I spent time alone with my daughter for the first time in awhile. I began to realize that my daughter is a truly wonderful child. She's fascinated by bugs I just kill and ignore. She looks at things and really sees them.

"Dad, doesn't that cloud look like Grandpa?"

"Not really dear, it needs some more fluff."

We colored, played games, went out to a restaurant, made cookies and ate ice cream. The highlight of the weekend came when my daughter made a card, decorated it with colors and put a phrase on the inside like only a five-year-old could, "Dad, ur a gd feand" translation, "Dad you're a good friend."

I know that no matter how far away my wife is she'll always be with us. I thanked her for enabling me to spend time alone with our daughter. From the five-year-old population of our house I'm now considered a hamburger-making, bath-giving and story reading expert. This is a distinction that gives me much pride. The weekend experience made me understand that I tend to spend too much time working. The time alone with my daughter made me realize that the most wonderful thing about being a father is actually having the chance to be a dad.

PROTECTIVE PARENTING

Strange and unexplainable things happen to a person when they have a child. Upon the first sight of their newborn infant a parent's heart rate increases and they feel all warm inside. Then a wave of determination comes over them to provide, protect and teach this beautiful little person about the many things they'll need to know in the world. It's one of the strongest emotions any person can experience.

Providing and teaching are the things that most parents seem able to keep in proper perspective. When it comes to the protect portion of having a child many parents can go a little bit on the insane side.

In an effort to protect their children from bacteria and germs some new mothers can start to act like a world leader involved in an armed struggle against the evil forces of germs and bacteria that have taken over their homes.

"Honey, you just disinfected the baby's room for the second time today. Why are you doing all this?"

"I shall clean the ceilings, I shall clean the walls, I shall clean from carpet to door. I will never surrender."

"I wish you would stop loading disinfectant into the squirt bottle and squirting me with it. Do you realize how really annoying that is when I'm in the bathroom?"

"Sorry, my dear husband. I have not yet begun to rid our home of germs and bacteria."

Something that can make any parent get crazy are all the things in the world that could cause physical harm to their children. These days when a child just tries to go out of the house for any reason their parents will give them a long list of instructions in the name of safety.

"Be careful when you go outside. Look both ways when you cross the street. Don't play with strange dogs. Don't talk to strangers. Call 911 if you see a fire, if anybody bothers you or your father tries to fix the cable by himself again. Put on your shoes and be careful where you step because broken glass could be anywhere. Don't forget to make sure both your shoes are tied even if you wear the slip-ons. Don't play with sharp objects. Don't hit anybody with a stick unless you have to and it's a good strong stick. Don't run with chewing gum in your mouth. Most of all be sure to have a good time."

"Mom, I'm just going down to the end of our driveway to the mail box to get the mail."

"Yeah, well, ah, be careful."

One of the main things parents try to protect their children from are hurt feelings. This is the one that seems very difficult as children are children and bound to upset one another. It doesn't really matter because the sight of their child being upset provides enough strong emotion in some parents to make them go a little berserk.

My daughter came home from playing one day. She was upset and crying. When my wife calmed her down she told us how one of the other kids she had been playing with said some mean things to her. It really hurt her feelings. I handled the matter in the same adult, mature way I handle everything that pertains to my daughter, I began screaming like a madman.

"I'll rip his head off. Don't worry sweetheart daddy will take care of this guy."

Before I made it to the door my wife grabbed me by the ear and dragged me back into the house.

"Mike, you're acting ridiculous. Kids do these sorts of things to each other."

"Then we'll sue him."

"He's only seven-years-old."

"So we won't get much but at least it'll teach him a lesson about hurting my daughter's feelings."

"Just calm down and listen to me. Kids sometimes say mean things to each other. I'll talk to his mother and maybe if the boy realizes he hurt our daughter's feelings he'll act different."

"And if he doesn't?"

"Then he doesn't. But our daughter has to learn to deal with things like this. You're not going to be able to watch over her every minute of every day for her entire life you know."

This realization caused me to feel a sharp pain in my chest as my heart started to break. I felt so very helpless. My lower lip popped out and I began to mumble.

"But, but, but. but."

"You're not going to do our daughter any good if you don't let her learn how to deal with life."

It's no fun when your spouse is right. As it turns out the boy came to our house, asked my daughter to play some more. My daughter told him what he said hurt her feelings. The boy was a good kid and said he was sorry and that she really didn't smell worse than a dead frog. He asked her again to go back out to play on the swings in his yard. I was amazed to discover that apologizing to females for bad behavior seems to start so young with guys. My daughter smiled as they left together and all was well in our world.

We parents sometimes have a desire to wrap our children in a protective cocoon that will keep them safe from all harm. We do our best and it's difficult to accept that we are mere mortals who can't provide such a cocoon for our children. Realizing we don't control everything in the world that could harm our child is one of the many things that make worrying an unspoken rule of parenting.

B-DAY

People who've entered the realm of parenthood often develop an overwhelming desire to make their child happy at any cost. In pursuit of seeing that special look of joy on their child's face many parents are willing to climb the highest mountain, swim the deepest ocean or even invite their child's friends over for a birthday party.

During a child's early years birthday parties are very popular social events that exist mainly for the parents of the child's friends. Parents bring their children to these infant parties, watch them spill things, fill their diapers and be very uninterested in anything going on around them except the dog's food dish or the cat's litter box.

When children enter the next birthday phase they've shed their diapers and unlocked the deep mysteries of bathroom usage. This is the time when parents drop their children off at the birthday child's home. Driving away with smug expressions these parents may burst into uncontrollable laughter. They probably just had their child's birthday party a few weeks earlier and know exactly what experiences await the host parents.

I tried to prepare for my daughter's birthday party like we were expecting an invasion force from a foreign army.

"Face paints."

"Check."

"Sidewalk chalk."

"Check."

"Pin the Tail on the Donkey game."

"Check."

"What would we need with an escape helicopter?"

"I don't want to take any chances."

On B-Day the first wave of little girls arrived in our driveway at the agreed upon time. They first encountered face paints, lawn games and sidewalk chalk. At that time my wife and I were doing a pretty good job at containing the children's attention span to the things we'd planned. When the next wave of little girls hit

31

our driveway they attacked the lawn games and face paints while the first group began to get a little bored.

That's when things started to look bad for our side.

Bored little children don't just sit around and wait for something to happen. These industrious individuals take it upon themselves to find some sort of entertainment whether it's allowed or not. They will pick flowers from your garden that should not be picked, turn on your lawn hose when it's not supposed to be turned on and if all else fails they will fight with each other.

"Don't call me stupid."

"Okay you're not stupid. You're ugly."

"I hate you."

"Oh yeah, well I hate you worse."

"I want to go home."

"Me too."

"Waaaah."

"Waaaah."

At those moments I did what any self-respecting father would have done, I asked my wife what to do next.

"It looks like we're being overwhelmed. Should we retreat to the back yard and call in the rescue chopper?"

"No, just get a book and I'll read to them."

"Shouldn't we call in the children's entertainment SWAT team or something?"

"No, just get a book."

"You're just going to read a book to the children?"

"Only after I hit you with it."

During B-Day my wife and I seemed to have two distinctly different roles. My wife was the chief negotiator during the event. She handled all arguments between the children with the skill of a UN ambassador. She also organized the games, fixed the refreshments and decorated the house. My role required that I ask my wife what to do next and give the children precise directions to the bathroom. We were an unbeatable team.

Our daughter was the perfect hostess. She carefully stacked all the presents her friends brought her in one area and informed us every five minutes that she was ready to open them.

"Is it time to open them yet?"

"Sweetheart your friends have only been here ten minutes."

"How about we open them in five more minutes."

"We've got a lot of things to do first."

"Six more minutes."

"How about you let me show you where the bathroom is?"

"Are there any more presents in there for me?"

We gave the children everything we had at the birthday party. There were games, cake and ice cream, present openings, more games, refreshments, unexpected games and little kids running everywhere.

By the end of the day our house looked like it had been hit by Hurricane Little Kid Birthday Party. My wife and I were exhausted. When the parent's started to arrive we treated them like liberating heroes.

"You have no idea how happy we are to see you."

"Quit kissing my hand."

The results from the polling the birthday party participants was positive. They couldn't wait for our daughter's birthday party next year, so they could tear up our yard, argue and ruin our flowers once again. I suppose we should be glad we're able to give them something to look forward to.

The celebration of my daughter's birthday is more than just a party for us. It is a time when we remember that special moment several years ago when we were blessed with a child. An event that has forever changed our lives. A milestone worthy of all the happy celebration we give it. The day when my wife and I changed from being just a couple, to being a family of our very own.

FIRST GRADE FOLLIES

I can remember the exact day my daughter started attending first grade. Parents of new first graders quickly discover that this is a very traumatic time in their child's life. The old days of part time learning are over and the child is now expected to attend full-day school. The teaching institution is suddenly restructured and the children's titles go from part-time kindergarten attendee to full-time non-exempt student.

Like many of her classmates my daughter handled this new challenge with all the grace and poise possessed by many first grade students. She constantly cried.

During the first few days of school my daughter's teacher listened to a serenade of crying children. They were a very expressive group telling the teacher about their strong desire to go home and informing her of their preference to be with their families instead of with her.

For her part the teacher handled the situation with a wealth of patience, understanding and professionalism. I was extremely impressed with the teacher. If it would've been me in that same situation I'm sure I would've required the consumption of heavy doses of tranquilizers even after being institutionalized.

In my daughter's grade school the children are disciplined by giving them something called a "time out." A "time out" is when the misbehaving child is removed from the class's activity for a specified period of time. The next step is the possibility of losing a certain amount of time to participate in outside recess.

This is in sharp contrast to what I experienced during the beginning of my primary education. We were all pretty motivated to pay attention in class and do what the teacher asked because of a strong desire to avoid experiencing pain.

My first grade teacher was a Yardstick Samurai. She could jump up, spin around, discipline four children, pass out assignments and collect everyone's milk money before she landed. I don't know if her methods helped me learn any better but I did develop a rather distorted view of yardsticks.

As everyone tells me, things were different back then.

The big event of first grade is learning how to read. I was shocked to learn that Dick, Jane and Spot are no longer a part of the first grade school experience. I guess it couldn't last forever. I'm sure that Dick is probably working for some

Fortune 500 company right now. Jane probably owns her own business and Spot is probably involved in dog food commercials and living in Malibu. Let's face it they were a gifted group. Nobody could watch each other run or run themselves quite like they could.

My daughter did well during her first grade experience. When she came home one day my daughter told me she felt she was having a little trouble trying to learn something in school and was upset. I saw this as a golden opportunity to give her a father-to-daughter type talk and put my dad skills to the test. It would be an uplifting parental lecture where the child would be transformed from being hopelessly upset over something into a super kid who feels so confident and secure they go out and may actually remember some of what you talked about five minutes later.

I put my arm around my daughter as she looked up at me intently.

"Don't be upset. It's all right if you don't do well in a certain subject. Your mom and I will help you the best we can and don't forget we will love you no matter what happens."

I felt good. She was still giving me this intent stare and even nodded her head in agreement.

"The only thing that really matters is that you try your best."

Now it felt like I was making a real difference in my daughter's life. Her eyes hadn't left me and I was surely destined for a Nobel Prize in fatherhood.

"So don't you worry about a thing. You'll be in school a long time and we'll be with you. Do you understand what I'm saying?"

She still gave me that intent stare and then smiled.

"Gee Dad, I just noticed you have nose hairs growing into your mustache. That's really neat."

Now I felt like an idiot, was looking for a hole to crawl into and thought I'd receive the Dopey Dad Award.

My daughter starting first grade was such a special day for my wife and me.

When our daughter left the house that first day I didn't see a six-year-old girl walk out of the door. At first I saw a helpless baby girl in a crib looking around in awe at all the things seen for the first time. Then the vision changed to a seven-month-old child crawling across our kitchen in an effort to catch the cat. The image turned into one of a pudgy legged toddler wobbling a little as she walked and showing her first two front teeth whenever she smiled. I saw the first hair cut, the first Christmas, the first time reciting the alphabet and first time swimming. I realized that before I know it the little girl I was looking at would forever change like the little baby I had once known.

I can remember as a kid not understanding the emotional expressions on my parent's faces or how they acted on the day I left for first grade. For some reason it now all makes perfect sense.

TRANSFORMATION TO GRANDPARENT

When I was growing up my father was always consistent as snow in winter and rain in summer. His routine was so predictable his nickname could've been Old Faithful. I really believe that if a foreign army had ever taken over our country when I was a kid my dad wouldn't have noticed until he couldn't play his Saturday golf game.

"Why don't you funny talkin' guys just get them there tanks off the green so I can play my game. I got a weekend pass y'know."

The only unpredictable behavior my father engaged in was the creation of swear words when fixing the family car. Most frustrated people can attach a regular word with a profanity and make a funny phrase but my dad refined this activity into an art form. He once changed the brakes on our car and his ingenious use of profanity with regular speech was worthy of a Pulitzer Prize. A small crowd formed around him while he worked and when he was finished they all applauded. It was an experience everyone in the neighborhood talked about for years.

This is the man I remember, rock-solid, steady and unchangeable. I don't know what happened to that guy because the man who is now my father has changed. I think it may be possible space aliens abducted my real father, took him to the planet Grandparent and implanted a computer chip in his brain. The person I know now couldn't be the same guy who raised me.

This impostor who claims to be my father has developed a unique ability to understand my daughter's behavior.

"Your granddaughter burned down our house and caused a riot today."

"Well, sometimes kids burn down houses and cause riots. I think your cousin did that when you guys were growing up. Don't be too tough on her she's just a kid y'know."

Is this the same man who thought I would have a career of a homeless person when I got a "C" on a report card for Biology? The teacher wanted me to touch dead things and even cut them open. It was pretty awful. This person can't be the same man who didn't understand my Biology dilemma.

My dad recently took my daughter to a video arcade and they were 20 minutes late returning. When they came in the house I looked at my father with my hands on my hips and gave them both very a very stern look.

"I want to know why you were late mister and it better be good."

Looking down and nervously moving his feet my dad said, "We just got busy an' forgot what time it was an' stuff."

In the deep recesses of my mind I remember experiencing a very similar situation but some how this one was extremely different.

If the word money floats from my daughter's mouth my father pulls out his wallet faster than a gun fighter from the old west taking out his pistol.

This is not the same man from my youth who felt Ebenezer Scrooge knew how to handle money. The mere mention of any desire for money just because I wanted it would cause my father to launch into graphic detail of his childhood struggles.

He had to work 26 hours a day starting when he was only four cells old. Before walking 200 miles to school in an Arctic blizzard he had to milk every cow in North America, feed the entire world population of chickens, plant enough crops to feed a few third world nations while only earning four cents a year. The most amazing thing is that he didn't even live near a farm.

I decided to confront my father about his drastic change in behavior. He then started talking to me like he was a prosecuting attorney.

"Wasn't it you who when a child would ask for candy from your grandparents when I told you not to?"

"Yeah, well…"

"Isn't it a fact that your grandparents bought you things for no reason other than they loved you?"

"I suppose so, but…"

"Do you deny your grandparents took you to the movies, gave you money and always took time to be with you?"

I yelled, "All right I confess, my grandparents spoiled me."

"Now then, wouldn't you say it is my turn to spoil my grandchild like my son was spoiled?"

"You're right."

"I rest my case."

As he sauntered away I wondered if Clarence Darrow ever talked to his son like this.

Grandparents are very important. The memories and lessons you get from grandparents have a value that can never be accurately calculated. The only thing more wonderful than having grandparents is the possibility of some day making the transformation to one yourself.

FOOD FIGHTING

When a child is first born eating is a rather simple event. The baby cries and its personal servants otherwise known as parents quickly get some nourishment and put it in the child's mouth. The baby eats, burps and goes to sleep. Not always in that order but usually with all these elements.

A necessary skill for survival with a newborn is a parent's ability to quickly learn their child's eating facial expressions.

The most important one is the "Whoa, I'm full and any more and I could erupt like a volcano."

Parents quickly realize this look is a serious situation because a baby will make good on the eruption threat.

The next phase is when kids get to experience something called solids. Children love this stage of life. It's a special time when parents display their acting talents and provide their child with an improv dinner show. Acting like lunatics, parents feel this is what is getting their child to eat.

Slowly a spoon full of food is flying around the baby's head as the parent makes a rather bizarre expression and says, "Here comes Mister Airplane. Varooom, right into the big baby's mouth."

Sometimes children will eat out of pity for their parents. There are other times the child will close its mouth, turn away and hope no other babies can see these people. They sit in their high chairs and wonder if their parents realize just how embarrassing the baby world finds such behavior.

When children begin to feed themselves they usually get an even proportion of food on themselves, on the floor and inside their clothing. Some of it even makes it into their mouths. At this point food is not only something they eat, it's also a fashion statement.

"Oh, look he's covered with green pea stuff."

"Here, let him eat some strawberry stuff and it will give him that holiday motif look."

"Okay."

Discovering what young children like to eat is very simple. If the child tries it, gags, sticks out its' tongue and threatens a lawsuit if it's ever fed that stuff again, it's a good sign the child doesn't like that particular food. If the child holds the parents hands to eat everything on the spoon, grabs for the bowl and threatens a lawsuit if it doesn't get more of that food you know the child likes that particular dinner. Parents should instantly add these items to their family-dining menu.

The next stage is when the child has developed an ability to speak and in-depth discussions follow every meal.

"Wan' 'tato chips."

"No, you're getting raisins."

"Wan' 'tato chips."

"I said no because you're getting raisins."

"Will constantly say wan' 'tato chips for the next several hours until you're on the verge of a nervous breakdown and give in to my desires."

"How about raisins and potato chips?"

"K Mommy."

I can remember when my daughter had reached the stage in her life where she hated to eat anything that didn't have the word hamburger, french fry or spaghetti in it. Mealtime was more than a time to eat, it was a time to engage in great culinary debates on the merits of what had been made for dinner.

"Sweetheart, you haven't even tried the stew I made. I want you to at least try it."

"I don't like it."

"How do you know you don't like it if you haven't tried it?"

Unfazed by my wife's common sense approach to things my daughter carefully takes her fork, removes about one molecule of food from the plate and then brushes it across maybe a single taste bud on her out stretched tongue.

"See, I tried it and I don't like it. It's awful."

My wife who is usually an easy-going and pleasant person begins to change. Like I'm watching the transformation scene in some werewolf movie my wife's face gets red, her body becomes rigid and she begins to speak in strange and unusual ways.

"You, ah, didn't even try it, you, ah, oooh, I ought to, you, ah, not making anything else, urrrr."

When my wife is very upset about my daughter's mealtime stubbornness she will look at me and I just begin to babble like a criminal trying to prove his innocence to the police.

"Hey, I ate my stew. I think it's good. I'll probably have seconds. Honest. I'm telling the truth. I swear."

After this experience I let my wife know that telling our daughter she can't have dessert until she turns forty might be considered a bit harsh. She assures me that if our daughter starts eating what's made for dinner she'd probably be able to have some dessert by the time she turns thirty.

After a certain amount of threats, negotiating and being told she won't be able to play with her friends until she eats, my daughter usually finishes dinner to my wife's satisfaction.

I suppose if children did everything just like their parents told them these parents would either check birth records to make sure they had the right kids or look for signs for alien implants. Children are always trying to make their own choices even when it comes to what they eat for dinner.

My wife and I slowly learned that the mealtime battles were more about my daughter taking control of some aspect of her life than actually not wanting to eat. It took time for our daughter to slowly get more control over other aspects of her life and then the eating became less of an issue.

Every child is different and they all give their parents different challenges. In a family mealtime changes over the years just like all its members. In time what the parents and children are eating doesn't become as important as the fact that they're all taking the time to eat together as a family.

COMMUNICATION CODE

The evolution of children and their parents not being able to properly communicate is a very common occurrence that has been taking place since the beginning of time.

William Tell once told his son "Get me the apple from the stand next to my bed and get me some tea. I want to practice shooting an arrow or two."

At that time William Tell's son was noticing a rather beautiful maiden who was winking and waving to him. This had the same effect on his young son as it does on all young men. The boy was in his own world with the maiden and had no idea he even had a father at the moment. If there were words spoken to him they were simply background noise as he admired the maiden.

William Tell was a man of little patience. He had no memories of being a young man enchanted by a beautiful maiden. William quickly became very annoyed with his son not paying attention to what he had just said and began yelling.

"Do it now or else."

The son was startled back to reality by his father screaming at him. He could only remember something that sounded like "Put the apple on your head and stand over by the tree. I want to practice shooting arrows at you."

This made no sense to the boy but he did it anyway to please his father. William Tell vented his frustration by shooting the apple off his son's head. To this day the father remains a hero and the son will always be remembered as a really confused young man.

One of the main reasons children and their parents miscommunicate is because parent's talk to their children in parent language and children listen to what they're told in child language. These are two very different and distinct interpretations of the same spoken words.

If a parent walks into a room and tells their six-year-old child "It's time for bath, go get your pajamas and clean underwear and put them in the bathroom."

The parent feels they've communicated very clearly what they want the child to do. Something very mysterious happens when the child hears these exact same words, because they sound very different to the six-year-old mind.

What the child hears is "Start coloring a picture of something right now and beg to finish it before bath. When that's over go to your bedroom and start playing with toys until your mother tells you to get pajamas and underwear at least three times. This is when you should run around the house trying to get the pet to chase you. When Mom's face gets so red she seems about to explode like a volcano it's time to submit to the bath but only right before you're threatened with no television."

Maybe interpreters could be used.

There are moments when parents and children communicate with no verbal exchange. A young child doing the "have to go to the potty dance" and refusing to go to the bathroom can give looks of extreme desperation as if they're on a reality television show. They want to be big enough to go without being told but they're not quite there yet. Mom will then ask if the child could test the bathroom to see if it's still working. With ego intact the child then bolts into the bathroom.

Parents who know no language other than parent tend to get frustrated with their children. When a child asks for a snack this parent will think of something just loaded with vitamins, minerals and designed to keep their child healthy until the kid is least 190-years-old.

The child who asked for the snack isn't too concerned with health. They're thinking of something with fat, grease and flavor that could clog the arteries of a blue whale in a very short time.

"Here's your snack, honey."

The child looks at the fruit and vegetables and gives the parent a look of total disbelief.

"Mom, this isn't what I wanted. I wanted corn chips."

The parent thinking in parent gives the child a look that communicates the idea he doesn't live in a restaurant and she is not his personal waitress.

"Well that's what you're getting."

"But Mooooooooom."

"Don't start with me. That's your snack, now eat it."

Once the mother is out of the room the child gets his best friend the dog to consume his snack. When mom comes back in the room it's gone and she smiles.

"That wasn't so bad, now was it?"

The child then smiles even more.

There are many ways parents communicate with their children that can never be accurately measured. It's the forced grin at the muddy footprints on a clean floor following a proud child holding freshly picked flowers for Mom. It's sharing the joy of learning how to tie a shoe or getting that big kid puzzle done. It's wiping away the tears from a bad fall or from being called a bad name. It's the importance placed on fixing a broken teddy bear. It's hugs and kisses upon demand and even that special time to cuddle.

It's seeing "I love you" in the child's eyes without it ever having been said. It's very important for children and parents to always communicate their loving feelings effectively. Once that's mastered everything else they say to one another has a chance of being understood.

YE OLE YARD SALE

My wife and I recently held something at our house called a yard sale. I've come to realize that yard sales are lovely events where people sell things that have been occupying space in their house for so long spiders have built cob web retirement homes on them.

The main goal of everybody holding a yard sale is to put as much useless stuff as possible on a lawn in hopes of finding someone who will fork over cold, hard cash for their junk.

The result of a yard sale is that the sellers no longer have an over abundance of items collecting dust in their house and now have enough money to go out and buy other things to clutter their homes and collect dust.

It's a viscous cycle.

When I was informed about our planned yard sale I thought that the whole thing should be handled like a professional business venture. I wanted to have an elaborate marketing campaign consisting of ads in all the local media, distribution of flyers and maybe a billboard advertisement. I even planned to contact a Hollywood agent in hopes of a possible celebrity endorsement.

My wife's idea on how to inform the world of our yard sale consisted of putting the words "Yard Sale" on two pieces of cardboard with arrows pointing toward our house. She'd put one on the telephone pole at one end of the street and one on the stop sign on the other end of the street.

Due to severe budgetary restraints my wife's marketing plan is the one we decided to use.

It almost seemed as if we'd built a baseball diamond in a Kansas cornfield, because they came.

People from all over the world or who at least lived four blocks away came to see the treasured mementos we were willing to part with for a price.

The negations were just as tough as any that take place on Wall Street.

"How much do you want for this eight track tape player that only plays one track?"

"That priceless family heirloom has been passed from generation to generation since the 1970s and has an emotional attachment that would be difficult to put a price on."

"I'll give you ten bucks."

"I'll throw in this complete eight track collection of the Bee Gees and a Bobby Sherman poster."

"Eleven dollars."

"Sold."

I'm sure we were the envy of corporate negotiators everywhere.

For anyone who thinks that people who buy things at yard sales are just individuals that happen to come across them could not be more wrong. I'm now certain there is a secret society of stuff buyers that scour the earth in search of stuff from yard sales for some reason unknown to mankind. The only proof I have of this is that my wife was selling things at our yard sale that she had bought at other yard sales.

The members of this society always dress as regular people, recognize the things they sold and are still willing to buy them. If you try to learn about this secret society you are met with strong resistance. I asked my wife a question about it and she started to speak in strange and unusual ways.

"Why are these people buying stuff you bought at a yard sale a few months ago?"

"Because, well, see, I saw it and now they see it and who knows maybe they'll use it or sell it or give it away and it's nice to get it and it could look nice wherever they put it."

Military intelligence probably couldn't break this elaborate code.

I've come to realize it wasn't a quest for monetary wealth that gave us a desire to have a yard sale. It was more a need to let go of some things from the past.

I did experience mixed emotions about parting with the white, wicker bassinet that sat solemnly on the grass. There was a time when the bassinet was used to rock our newborn baby girl to sleep. As I looked at it I thought about when our daughter was small enough to be in the bassinet and how my wife and I felt so much joy just watching her sleep.

It had done its job well for us and I felt certain that there was another newborn somewhere who could use it.

On the other side of the yard was an old wooden chair. My wife and I bought it when we were newlyweds and placed it in our sparsely furnished apartment. At that time in our lives nothing mattered to us but being with each other every minute of every day.

The chair had served its desired purpose over the years and seemed more like an old friend than a wooden object. I was sure someone could find a use for it other than to collect dust in the corner of a basement.

It was a difficult experience to part with these items but it seems that part of my life is past. The bassinet and old wooden chair may be gone but I know all the special memories I associate with them will last me a lifetime.

AGELESS UNDERSTANDING

It had been one of those days that felt like the world was giving me an emotional endurance test. A really lousy one where you're not even aware of how much the negative feelings have wrapped their tentacles around you and are squeezing every thought in your brain. I came home from work after having had just such a bad day and made the mistake of bringing too much of the frustration home with me. I was quite unhappy with everybody and everything in my path.

When I'm very upset I always display some rather unique and identifiable behavior. I will begin talking in partial sentences and have no idea why everyone isn't aware of what I'm talking about or why I'm upset. Combine this with my sighs and how I start to pace around while constantly rattling the keys in my pants and you'll understand why my wife's been considered for sainthood during our marriage.

When I came through the door on that awful day it took my wife about two seconds to realize I was not in a good mood.

"What's the matter?"

"Yeah, well, I don't know why it has to be me. I'm tired of it and some things have to change is all I'm saying."

"What are you talking about?"

"Oh, like you don't know. I told you before and it's the same as always only this time it's a little worse. Don't know how much more I can take. I'm telling you that right now."

My wife looked at me and let out a sigh as she quickly walked out of the room. I know she claimed to be going to finish making dinner, but I think she was actually getting the phone to call a "Wives of Husbands in a Bad Mood" hotline.

At dinner it became apparent my daughter had also experienced a bad day. She didn't complain about what we were having for our meal so I knew something was wrong. She didn't try to sell us on the idea of visiting her favorite fast food restaurant or even try to negotiate the early release of her dessert. This dinner was unlike any other we'd had in a long time.

When my daughter came to the table she sat down, sighed and started talking in partial sentences.

"What's the matter?" my wife said.

"You know, usual stuff. My friend left me at recess, played with someone else, teacher got mad, wasn't my fault, spilled my milk at lunch, messed up an assignment and couldn't find my favorite pencil with the rubber dog eraser. Just the usual stuff. Something has to change I know that."

I think she may have actually tried to put her hand in her pockets in an attempt to rattle some toy keys.

When I looked down at my daughter I didn't feel like being understanding. I felt quite the opposite and my frustration bubbled to the top and burst.

"Boy I wish I had your life. I think it would be great if all I had to worry about was teachers and spilling milk. Hey, I even wish I had recess during my day. Wait until you get older and have bills to pay and have a boss to deal with. Then you'll really have something to be upset about."

I felt a little better but my daughter seemed a little worse. Her head sunk low as she turned away from me and let out another sigh. When I looked over at my wife she was busy giving me an "angry mom face" expression. This is the facial expression every mother comes equipped with that enables them to communicate misbehavior to their child with a single glance. I recognized this from my younger days and automatically responded like any innocent kid.

"What?"

My wife looked at me and began to let loose a string of words like she was some judge on an afternoon legal television program.

"Excuse me Mister, but I don't think you have an exclusive right to feeling upset. Our daughter's feelings are just as affected by what happens to her as yours are by what happens to you. As far as I'm concerned you've got no right to sit here and act like her feelings don't matter just because you have grown-up problems and she has little kid problems. Being an adult means you actually have to act like one once in awhile."

Things got very quiet at the dinner table.

I realized my wife was right. How many times do parents think their kids have no problems just because they're kids? I guess we have to realize problems are problems no matter what age we are and always have an affect on us.

Later I talked with my daughter alone in her room.

"Sweetheart, I'm sorry for how I acted tonight at dinner. I was upset with other things and not you. I'm sorry if I upset you."

My daughter smiled.

"That's all right Daddy. I know you love me a lot so you must have been really upset by something."

She came to me, gave me a hug and showed me a picture she was drawing.

I was very touched. When I looked at my daughter I realized forgiveness and understanding are very important to learn. I discovered they're actually two things that can easily be taught to you at any age.

TAX GIRL

The other day I was engaged in an annual event which causes me such serious mood swings I could put a menopausal female to shame. It's that agonizing time of year when I experience the torment of filing my end-of-year tax returns.

Each and every time I work on taxes my emotions run the gamut from elation, when it looks like I might be getting a tax return check, to a depression so bad I almost don't want to watch sports for an entire weekend. This depression usually happens when it looks like I'll have to write a check to the IRS or my favorite sports team has lost in the play-offs.

One day in April I was sitting at my desk wrapped in calculator tape and thinking of some rather nasty names for the IRS when I decided to take a break. I'd reached the grumbling stage of tax preparation and needed to give it a rest. My inquisitive daughter strolled into my office with a rather curious expression on her face.

She looked at me with a bright, cheery smile and said, "What are you doing Daddy and why are you grumbling so much?"

My instincts as a parent told me to view this situation as an opportunity to teach my daughter about the concept of paying taxes.

"Well whenever your daddy gets paid he has to give some money to people in the government to help run our country. He doesn't get to say who gets the money he gives to the government but just has to fork over his hard-earned cash no matter how it makes him feel. The government doesn't care if he likes it or not."

I thought I'd made my point rather well but then my daughter hit me with the mother of all children's sayings.

"Why?"

"Because this is how we pay policemen to protect us from bad guys and firemen to help us in case we have a fire at our house. We also have to give money so all the politicians we elect to run the government can get together and vote themselves a pay increase every year."

"If we don't have a fire or call a policeman do they give us our money back?"

"No, they most certainly do not."

"Why?"

I was about to lecture some more when I realized I was talking to a small child.

"Because they don't."

"What if you don't pay them money."

"Then they come and take it from you and make you wish you would have given it to them in the first place."

"That's not fair."

"Yes, but that's the way it is."

"Why?"

I was trapped. My daughter had unknowingly just committed one of the biggest mistakes known to man, trying to make sense out of how the tax system works. This was a very crucial moment. My mind pondered the possibility of describing the complex concept of taxation to a first grader or taking a more basic approach any child could understand. I opted for the latter.

"Because there is a big monster that lives deep inside the earth named Zorg. If we don't pay taxes Zorg will come up to the surface and devour all the children's toys until there aren't any left to play with."

She thought about that one for a minute and shrugged her shoulders.

"That doesn't make any sense."

"Well, ah, you better let me finish doing the taxes because I don't think you want to take any chances with your toys."

"Daddy, you're being silly."

"Hey, don't worry about it then. You're the one with all the toys around here that could get eaten."

My daughter looked at me for a second and then ran to her bedroom. I think I heard the sound of her hiding toys for some reason.

When it comes to the annual tax event my wife has learned not to say a word to me. She sees what a mood I'm in and will stand at a safe distance away and carefully throw bits of food into my office to help sustain me. When I finally file our tax returns calm reappears in our home. When I'm finished with the taxes my wife will only utter two sentences to me.

"If they're wrong you're the one who's going to jail" and "Just show me where I sign."

My wife's system frustrates me at times but it seems to do her very well.

My daughter came back later and saw I was still working on the taxes. I had left the grumbling stage and had entered the grunting, slamming the pencil on the desk phase. She just stood there looking at me and not making a sound.

When I turned my chair around to face her she came to me and gave me a big hug.

"What's that for sweetheart?"

"I decided to give all my toys to that Zorg monster thing."

"Why is that?"

"Well I figure if I give him all my toys you won't be so upset by doing this tax stuff and you can be happy again."

I hugged my daughter tightly and looked for a tissue.

Sometimes when parents think they have a chance to teach their children something new, it's actually the parents who end up doing all the learning.

MYSTERY GROWING

All parents share one very common experience when it comes to having children. It's a phenomenon that most of us deal with every day of our parenting lives. It's something called "Mystery Growing."

When we see our children one day we wonder when they'll ever get rid of that pacifier. The next day we are shocked to find they want to drive the car to school. We see them change on a day-to-day basis and yet aren't able to pinpoint the exact moment that new tooth came in or when they figured out thunder may not actually be caused by angels bowling.

Parents can very easily be caught unaware of the advances their children have made and refuse to acknowledge that a teenager has actually grown enough to sit at the grown-up table during holidays.

"Aw, Mom, I refuse to sit at the same table with my cousin Eddie. He always sticks food up his nose."

"He's your cousin and you did the exact same thing when you were his age."

"Mom, that was over ten years ago. I was a little kid then."

"And what are you now?"

"Old enough to learn how to drive."

"I'd rather you stick food up your nose."

"Mooooooom."

Without my knowledge or permission our daughter has engaged in a lot of mystery growing of her own. I became aware of this one day when she wanted a snack. When I reached to get her a bowl she informed me she could get her own bowl. I smirked and waited for her to get it and a glass from the cabinet over the stove. My daughter simply moved a chair over to the stove, got on top of it then got a bowl and glass from the cabinet. She also got herself chips, poured herself a drink and put the chair back.

It didn't stop with getting snacks. She was able to put her movies in the VCR and run them. She could take showers by herself and pick out her clothes for school. It didn't register in my mind how much progress she'd made in her life until the day I volunteered to help her get on her coat.

"Dad, I can do it myself. I'm not little any more."

It felt like I'd just swallowed a softball. She was right. I decided to talk this over with my wife.

"Our daughter has been growing up without my permission."

"What?"

"She's learning how to take care of herself and she didn't even ask us if she could do such a thing. We need to have a talk with her."

"For what? Being a healthy developing child?"

"Yeah. I bet if we work together we can put an end to this before it gets out of hand."

"Mike, she's not doing anything wrong."

"You think so? Next thing you know she'll learn how to play Parcheesi and then it's on to figuring out the mysteries of the Tooth Fairy. From there she'll progress to being able to remove those child safety caps and then we're in real trouble."

"Why? Because instead of depending on you to do things for her she'll be able to depend on herself?"

"You say that like it's something normal."

"It is normal. This isn't about her; it's about you isn't it?"

I opened my mouth but no words came out. My wife was right. I was feeling threatened by my daughter's independence. I'd always loved the feeling of being so needed by her that I was having trouble with her growing up.

I went into the room where my daughter was playing with stuffed animals. I looked at her and felt helpless, realizing I was no match for Father Time. Once our children are born they engage in a lifelong process of growing up and getting out on their own. That is something that will always be difficult to experience.

In a flash, I saw her finishing high school, graduating from college and getting married. I also saw me being able to be a part of her life for all those events. Maybe the only thing we can do as parents is to be there for our children so much that when they're older and don't need us they still want us in their lives anyway.

I went over to my daughter and when she looked up at me said, "Sweetheart, I'll always love you."

My daughter smiled. "I'll always love you too, Dad. Why did you say that?"

"Because I mean it sweetheart. I really mean it."

GOTTA' DANCE

Friend's of mine who have daughters told me it would happen to my daughter one day but I was still surprised when their prediction rang true. It happened when we were watching television and on the screen was a beautiful and graceful ballerina dancing. My daughter was mesmerized by this image. We then progressed from watching television to her asking for dancing videos. This led to the discovery of her friends taking dancing lessons and then the big moment happened. It occurred during dinner one night when my starry eyed daughter informed me she'd realized her life's vocation.

"Dad, I want to be a dancer. I want to move around to music and dress in pretty clothes."

"Would you like to take dance lessons?"

"My friends take those. What exactly are dance lessons?"

"Lessons are when a person who knows how to dance will teach you how to become a great ballerina."

My daughter didn't understand this concept of lessons. She thought she could already move around like a ballerina and wear pretty clothes with the best of them. I tried to explain that she couldn't just get on television or perform on big stages without taking lessons. Dance lessons would teach her how to do many of the amazing movements she liked to watch. Since she felt already endowed with many dancing talents my daughter reluctantly agreed to take these things called dancing lessons.

I soon discovered that dance teachers of little girls are empowered with more patience and understanding in one molecule of their body than I will have in a life time. I always assumed little girls would be anxious to line up and learn to dance. This is only true if you can get them to actually realize that the reason they're in that room is for dancing lessons and now is the time to learn about dancing.

When I started dropping my daughter off for her dance class I discovered little girls have many important things to do before they can even begin to pay any attention to the teacher. There is running around and screaming that has to be done. Slamming tap shoes on the floor louder than your friend is very important as well as laughing and giggling. When they're finished they've got to talk about school, complain about their siblings or brag about their new toys.

With a firm and gentle voice the dance teacher would tell the girls to line up. She would politely ask them to straighten the line and clap her hands to get their attention. With the skill equal to any disc jockey on the planet she would find a place on a record and beginning playing music. Carefully she would move her legs and arms to the beat of the music and assume that the girls would imitate her.

I looked at some expressions on the faces of the little girls and it seemed they had no idea what was happening.

Their little minds seemed to be filled with thoughts like "Why is that lady in front of us moving her leg? Oh yeah, she wants me to do the same thing. Now she's moving her arms and turning. Boy is this woman confused. I wonder what we're having for dinner?"

After the first lesson I asked my daughter what she thought. She grumbled. I then told her how things would get better with the next few lessons. She gave me a look of shock.

"You mean I have to go back there again?"

"Yes, you're going back once a week for the entire school year. At the end of the year they have a big show and you'll be able to dress in pretty clothes and dance on a stage like you wanted."

"Can't I just go and do that dress in pretty clothes and dance stuff at the end of the year?"

"No."

"I don't want to go to dance lessons."

"We paid good money for those lessons. You agreed to do this and you're going."

I always wondered where my wife developed such an ability to give me angry expressions. After seeing the look my daughter's face I realized women start developing this angry expression ability when they're very young.

Dance lessons slowly developed into a weekly battle. My daughter would lose things, my wife and I would find them. She then became rather imaginative in creating excuses not to attend dance lessons.

"I can't go to dance today. I'm developing a disease or something. Maybe I'm allergic to tap shoes."

"You're going."

"I think scientists have discovered dance lessons could be hazardous to your health. I think I shouldn't go to dance until all the research is done."

"Very creative, but you're going."

The day of the show parents, grandparents and relatives from all over made their way to the school auditorium. There were so many video recorders and cameras in the audience it looked like the president might be doing a dance.

All of the children were dressed in very pretty costumes and danced their best. You could sense the pride they had in themselves and determination to do well. They all did fantastic. When my daughter performed my wife and I smiled a lot and tightly held hands. Afterward we asked my daughter if she enjoyed herself and she informed us she really did love taking dance lessons. For some reason my wife and I both found the nearest wall and began to hit our heads against it.

My wife and I have always realized that having a child is something wonderful. It's a wild roller coaster ride of good and bad times. On a day-to-day basis parents do homework with their kids, make sure they eat right, cross the street safely and are taken care of in every way. They clean their children's clothes, take care of them when they're sick, dispense lunch money and are so involved with the many things that go into raising their children they don't have an opportunity to see any results of their child raising efforts.

The parents who watched their children dance that night felt a sense of pride and fulfillment. It's something parents often experience from being involved with their children and knowing in their heart that they played a part in the success of that beautiful child dancing so gracefully across the stage.

PARENTAL GROWING PAINS

My wife was going out with her friends one night and that meant I got to watch our daughter for the evening. It would be just the two of us and I was looking forward to spending some time alone with her. It'd been a while since we had spent time by ourselves and I planned to make things special. I planned such a wonderful evening I envisioned a father-daughter bonding experience that would be admired by every parental organization on the planet.

First we would play with her doll house. This would consist of me providing all the voices for each figure. The plastic father figure is a big hero and saves the mommy and daughter figures from the crazed plastic farm animal figures that come into the house making loud and bizarre noises. Adults may frown at this but for my child this has always been quality entertainment.

The evening festivities wouldn't end there. We would draw pictures and color them. She'd draw a picture of a beautiful princess and I'd probably make a picture of the burping dragon drinking seltzer water. In the past telling her about the burping dragon drinking seltzer water has caused my daughter to laugh so much she needed to make a mad dash for the bathroom.

After all that I would order pepperoni pizza. While we ate she'd ask me questions like how pepperoni was made, where it came from, why its name was pepperoni and why we put it on pizza. I'd handle those questions like any other stereotypical father. I'd just tell her to ask her mother.

The father-daughter event would end on a positive note with bedtime consisting of me reading stories and providing all her favorite voices from the grumpy panda voice to the silly snake voice and I knew she would just love all of this so much.

When she walked in the door from school I smiled and stood by her doll house.

"Well sweetheart, Mom is going out with her friends tonight. It's just you and me. How about we play with the ole' doll house?"

"No, I want to go play with my friends across the street."

Upon hearing those words I felt as if a wrecking ball had just hit me in the chest.

60

"What about the daddy saving the daughter and mommy from the farm animals making loud, bizarre noises?"

"We can do that another time."

A little girl appeared at my front step and asked my daughter to go and play. I told her it was all right and they left together.

As they walked away I yelled, "Next time the mommy and daughter in the doll house need saved from farm animals Daddy may not provide such great sound effects."

They both looked at me like I was crazy.

When my daughter returned for dinner I'd bought a large pepperoni pizza. She helped setting things up and then we sat down to eat. She told me about her friends, things they had planned, things they'd done in the past. She was quite excited about the clubhouse they were busy making.

"Don't you want to know anything about the pepperoni?"

"No, Mom told me all about it."

"Figures."

After dinner was over we cleaned up and I pointed to paper and crayons.

"Want to draw some stories?"

"No, I want to go across the street and work on the club house with my friend."

There was a knock on the door and the same little girl who lived across the street was asking for my daughter. I told my daughter it was all right for her to go and play.

As they were walking away I yelled "You can have your club house but I doubt you'll ever hear a story as good as the burping dragon drinking seltzer water. It's a timeless classic."

They giggled and ran away. I tried to not be disappointed but it was an uphill battle.

At bedtime I read a storybook to my daughter without much enthusiasm. The grumpy old panda voice and the silly snake voice both seemed depressed. It was obvious I wasn't feeling too happy. My daughter looked at me and knew something was wrong.

"What's the matter Dad?"

"I wanted to spend the whole evening alone with you. I missed you when you went over to your friends house."

"I know but sometimes I get tired of being at home and just want to go and play with other kids."

She was right. I was being selfish. She had grown to a point where she had her own friends, her own way of doing things, her own life. The realization of how much she had grown was hitting me like a ton of bricks. For some reason it just didn't seem fair.

"Do me a favor sweetheart."

"What Daddy?"

"Quit being so mature. If you're too mature before you become eighteen-years-old I'll lose you as a tax deduction."

"Huh?"

"Never mind."

She gave me a hug and a kiss then curled up under her covers. Before I closed her bedroom door that night I suddenly realized the days of her being a little girl were numbered.

When my wife came home I was busy sulking.

"What's the matter?"

"My days of playing with our daughter and making bizarre farm animal noises with the doll house, figures or drawing pictures of the burping dragon drinking seltzer water, or even listening to questions about pepperoni will be over soon. She now prefers to be with her friends."

My wife put her arms around me.

"She's growing up. She needs to be with other children. She's starting to get a life of her very own."

My lower lip stuck out and I shuffled my feet.

"It's just not fair."

"Oh, don't worry, she'll always love you. Just in a different way."

"How do you know?"

"Don't forget, I was once a little girl with a father who loved me more than anything."

It's strange how you can look at your child every day and know they're growing and changing. It's a completely different thing when you actually have a chance to experience it.

A LESSON FOR DAD

I have a friend who owns his own successful small business. Many times during the week he'll work a fourteen-hour day and for my friend that is quite normal. His business has done well and he has slowly gotten more spare time, which he likes to spend doing things with his family. His main topics of conversation on any given day are always his family. He likes to tell stories about teaching his kids how to swim or how to fish or the latest adventure of taking them camping. His desk is filled with their pictures and some very artistic child's drawings. He's the kind of guy who is always willing to share his children's achievements or pull out a wallet full of family pictures at any moment.

It was then very unfortunate that the day of the open house for his son's school was a bad time for him. His business was having some problems. One of his employees couldn't make it in because they were sick and an important customer decided to cut down the business they were doing with him. In the morning he had to park down the street because there were no parking spaces at his building where his office was located. Add all that to a computer crash and an order for supplies that wasn't even close to being right and you have one very stressed out father.

When he got home he was tired and in need of relaxation. At dinner his wife politely reminded him that they were going to the open house at their son's school. He groaned and said he was really tired and just didn't feel up to it tonight.

His ears were then serenaded from one very disappointed child.

"Aw, pleeeeeease Dad. Pleeeease, I really want you to go. I really want to show you my desk. We did some good stuff. You'll see. Pleeeeease go Dad, pleeeease."

After a sufficient amount of guilt had built up inside of him this dad finally gave in and agreed to attend the open house.

He was not in a pleasant mood by the time he got to the school. The first thing that happened is they couldn't find a parking spot near the school. It was so crowded with parents visiting the school they had to park pretty far away. The dad grumbled at all the cookies and punch that had been prepared for the night. He really wanted to be home relaxing rather than at the open house. He was silent and just looked at his watch when talking to his son's teachers. He sighed at all the artistic creations that adorned the school walls.

Finally the big moment came when they made it to his son's homeroom. Feeling very excited the son took his father's hand and led him to his desk. It appears that all of the children had to write an essay about someone that they wanted to be like when they got older. With a big wide smile that displayed heart-felt pride the son handed his father the essay he'd written.

The title of his son's essay was "Why I want to be just like my dad."

The essay told the story about how his son felt he had the best dad in the world. His dad was the best fisherman, best swimmer and camping guy in the whole wide world. The son told about how special it was to spend time with his dad. When he got old enough to have a child he was going to do all the fun thing with his kid that his dad had done with him.

The dad was a former combat officer in the military but looked like he didn't know exactly how to handle this situation. He looked away and gently wiped a tear from the corner of his eye.

Then the dad slowly leaned down and hugged his son and whispered in his ear "Thanks for the essay son. You did a good job and I really appreciate it."

His son's response was simple.

"It's easy to write stuff like that about you Dad because I love you and it's all true."

For some unknown reason after that the dad was no longer tired. He actually began to see all the wonderful artwork that adorned the walls of the school. He stopped and talked again with a few of the teachers. Before it was all over he actually had a cookie and some punch.

Sometimes it's easy for parents to forget how important they are to their children. Many dads may never win a sport's championship, lead troops to victory in a great battle or be a famous movie star but they can always be a big hero to that special little child in their life.

TO TELL THE TRUTH

One of the big things that goes with being a parent is teaching your children good values. A value that always gets a high rating on the important type value scale is telling the truth. Getting our children to always tell the truth is of such importance some parents are tempted to hook their children up to lie detectors whenever anybody's favorite stuffed animal turns up missing or the snack drawer is open during a no snack time.

We parents can give our child lengthy, fact-filled lectures about the virtues of telling the truth no matter what the situation. In the same breath and without feeling the slightest bit hypocritical we will then remind this same child not to forget to put their tooth under their pillow so they can get some money from the Tooth Fairy.

It makes perfect sense that we will tell our children there are no such things as monsters but there is a little creature that will fly into their room at night, as they sleep, to remove a discarded body part and leave them cold hard cash.

One of the things that was quite popular when I was growing up was the idea of the Sandman. I was not a big fan of this guy who allegedly put sand in your eyes to put you to sleep. For some reason the thought of some sandman guy coming into my room at night to put his special knockout sand narcotic in my eyes didn't appeal to me at all. This story not only did not help me get to sleep but had quite the opposite effect. It made me stay awake in fear waiting for this guy so I could be sure to get away from him. I would booby trap my room and hope nobody got too injured if they stepped on my strategically placed marble collection.

"Daddy, daddy I just saw the sandman."

"Don't be silly. You're still awake. Did you see him put sand in your brother's eyes?"

"No, I saw him go out the back window with the TV and stereo."

"Oh."

Another favorite is the Easter Bunny. Today children watch about 847 different nature shows per month and many tell the real story about woodland rabbits. Yet, parents are foolish enough to believe that their children buy into the concept that a woodland creature could get eggs, paint eggs and hide eggs for kids all around the world without even having a thumb. While doing this of course he never runs into the hungry Easter predator who seems to take vacation Easter day.

"Dad, this is a great Easter egg hunt. Do you really believe in the Easter Bunny?"

"You bet I do. Everybody knows he's a space mutant that scientists keep locked up in a secret government laboratory in Iowa."

"Daaaaaaaad."

"All right, all right."

Everybody's favorite has to be the idea of Santa Claus. The very popular and commercialized red-suited present-delivery elf from the North Pole. I can remember as a child having some serious doubts about this guy, but I didn't want to take any chances of not getting presents.

It was his naughty and nice intelligence network that upset me. Did he have KGB operative elves on his payroll or something? Did our parents, teachers or friends turn us in to Santa at the end of the year? Were some other kids selling me out to Santa so they could get a new bike and baseball glove?

This is why I usually started most of my letters to Santa Claus like:

"Dear Santa, I hope you see my side of the story when judging me for the piece of pizza that somehow got thrown onto my mother's new white kitchen curtains."

One year my friend considered having an attorney write his letter to Santa in order to better explain the garter snake in the sister's underwear drawer incident.

There is one main reason we parents lead our children to believe in these things, because we were led to believe in them when we were kids. We know what it's like to find that money under your pillow or the thrill of finding those hidden eggs. Everybody can probably remember the feeling of getting that one special gift on Christmas morning. These are special times when parents know what their children are feeling. It makes parents remember being a child and hope their own children will hold these moments so special they talk about them for a lifetime.

VACATION ANARCHY

I recently saw a friend of mine after he had just gotten back from vacation with his family. He'd taken his wife and three children on a car trip out of state to visit some relatives. They planned to stop along the way to visit a few attractions and thought this would probably be the best vacation they'd ever experienced.

When I went up to him at the store his hair was disheveled, his face had a few days growth of a beard and he had huge bags under his eyes. The most noticeable thing about him was the strong socially unacceptable aroma that emanated from his person. I tried to not let the fact I was holding my nose be too noticeable as I spoke to him.

"Hey, how did your vadation' go dis' year?"

He looked at me like an exhausted athlete, smiled and started to limp toward the store exit as he spoke.

"It was a good time. We'll get together and talk about it in a day or two."

As I watched my friend hobble out of the store he reminded me of a picture I once saw of Napoleon's troops retreating at Waterloo.

A few days later we got together for lunch and I was able to hear the sordid tale of his vacation adventure.

"It was a little rough because the cigarette lighter in the car didn't work."

"You and your wife don't smoke."

"No, but that's how we planned to power my son's computer game."

"Was it a big deal that your son couldn't play his computer games?"

"Yeah, because then he engages in his next favorite activity in life."

"What's that?"

"Teasing his sister."

"Oh."

He told me it's a true test of a father's self control to drive down the highway and listen to a serenade of fighting children. He told me senseless things come out of your mouth before you realize you've said them.

"He touched me."

"Quit touching your sister."

"She started it. She touched me first."

"Nobody touch anybody for any reason whatsoever. From now on the car is a no touching zone. Understand?"

My friend smiled at me and said he was glad their eighteen-month-old was in back with the two older kids.

"Why?"

"Oh, the baby stopped the other two when they were fighting."

"How did she do that?"

"She got car sick and threw up on them."

"Oh."

One of the stops they made was his aunt's place that was located in another state. She was in her late fifties and had never married or had children.

"How was the visit at your aunt's place?"

"It was all right. She spent a lot of the time gasping and telling the kids not to touch things. I think she was glad when we left. She hated to say good-bye to our youngest."

"She liked the baby?"

"No, she held our eighteen-month-old to say good-bye and I think the smell from my aunt's perfume didn't agree with the baby so our child got a little sick on the expensive jewelry she was wearing."

"Oh."

They then traveled to his wife's parent's home.

"How was that?"

"It was great. I ate a lot of good stuff, drank a lot of good stuff, stayed up too late and really didn't get much sleep. The only problem is I tried to do our laundry when we were there and ended up shrinking and changing the color on a few things."

"How did your wife handle that?"

"She banned me from unsupervised laundry washing for life."

"Oh."

After that they left to head home and stopped at Sea World.

"How was that?"

"That was really a lot of fun until my eight-year-old daughter and ten-year-old son made each other get sick."

"How did they do that?"

"You can buy these dead fish to feed the dolphins. When my daughter laughed at something my son put a dead fish in her mouth."

"That's awful."

"My daughter was not to be out done. She saved some of the dead fish and put them on my son's hamburger when we were eating."

"Oh."

"After that everything was going fine until we left and got in the car. Our youngest started screaming because we didn't have her pacifier."

"What did you do?"

"The people at Sea World were kind enough to let me back in and look for it. I found it in the bathroom and rushed with it to the car like a doctor heading for a dying patient."

"No problems after that?"

"We had a flat tire on the drive home. When my son got out to help me we let the car down too soon and it scraped my leg. I limp a little now but it'll get better. We were all glad to get home because we were so tired."

"Sounds like a rough vacation?"

My friend looked at me and smiled.

"Naw, it wasn't too bad. We got to do everything together and that's what made it fun."

He was right. I guess there's no experience in life so bad it can't be made easier by just going through it together as a family.

CAFETERIA WOES

School cafeterias are wonderful places located in the schools where we send our children to become educated. Every day we give our children either a bag lunch or money to buy a lunch at the school cafeteria. We parents live under the assumption that the cafeteria is a place where our children go to enjoy their noon time meal. We parents have visions of them eating their food, talking and leaving in an orderly fashion when they're finished.

We parents live in a dream world.

The reality is that all children go to the school cafeteria to talk, complain about food, attempt to gross each other out and try to get away with throwing food at each other. On a very rare occasion they actually do something like eat.

There are usually two different factions in the cafeteria, bag lunchers' and school lunch buyers. When I was growing up I saw the many benefits to being a bag luncher'. The school lunch buyers all had pretty much the same food but I could take different things every day. I put this to my advantage when I wanted to trade something from my lunch for something a school lunch buyer would have.

At times like this we were like stock brokers negotiating trades on Wall Street. We would skillfully bargain portions of our lunches to each other.

"Hey, I'm talkin' all beef bologna sandwich here. Talk ta' me. Tell me what ya' got?"

"Cafeteria Brownie."

"Cafeteria Brownie? We don' do that with all beef bologna. That's for cheese puff days. Get serious, will ya'?"

"Cafeteria Brownie and my chocolate milk."

"Throw in a coupla' yer' fries there an' we got ourselves a deal."

"Done."

Every cafeteria on the planet is required to have lunch ladies. These highly experienced females are the cafeteria version of policewomen. During lunch they patrol throughout the cafeteria holding sponges to wipe up spills and reminding kids to behave. When one kid gets out of line about a thousand lunch ladies from

70

all over the country come and crowd around the misbehaving child and bombard him with questions.

"Don't leave without taking your tray up, mister."

"Hey, it's not my tray."

"What do you mean not your tray? I saw you eating the food off of it."

"I'm a bag luncher'. See, here's my bag."

Using the international lunch lady signal for reinforcements by nodding her head toward the unruly kid, even more lunch ladies appear to confront the child.

"Why can't you take the tray up anyway?"

"Well, I…"

"How would you like us to talk about your behavior with your teacher?

"The principal?"

"Your parents?"

"The president?"

"The UN Secretary General?"

"Huh?"

"There was a kid your age named Elmer who didn't take a tray up like we asked and he ended up becoming a criminal and now is sitting in prison for the rest of his life. He'd have turned out quite different if he would've just taken up a tray like we asked."

"All right, all right already, I'll take up the tray."

As the child takes the tray and walks toward the exit they've learned one very valuable lesson in school cafeteria survival, don't mess with the lunch ladies.

What occurs during my daughter's school lunch experience is always a mystery to my wife and I. It seems that something happens with her mid-day meal that causes selective amnesia. We've sent her to school with a bag lunch, only to have her return with it untouched. We ask her what she ate for lunch and she doesn't know. She ate something but wasn't sure what it was. We've given her money to buy lunch at the school and when we asked what she had to eat she doesn't know, but it was something. We know she's eating because the stains on her clothes are from some kind of food. Recently, we sent her to school with a lunch we packed and she returned with her lunch bag containing a completely different set of untouched food. I don't know if we should talk to the school or contact the FBI Mystery School Lunch Division.

My wife and I sometimes share stories with our daughter about when we were in school. Lunch ladies, the food, friends and events that seem to repeat themselves for generations. It's nice to share your growing up experiences with your kids. It gives parents a chance to remember a time when they weren't adults and gives their children a chance to think about their moms and dads as being young. They realize their parents were at one time actual kids just like them, but now it's their turn to go down a common path their parents have already traveled.

PET PEEVES

My wife and I decided the time had arrived in our daughter's life for another step toward maturity. It would be a major milestone and one we felt our daughter was at last ready to experience. We were going to get her a pet.

We talked about the wonderful things having a pet could teach our daughter and decided it would be a good idea. We felt she could develop a sense of responsibility by learning how to properly feed and care for a living creature. This might also stop her constant complaining about her friends having pets and the extreme depravation she feels by not having one.

We thought if we handled this one experience properly it would probably mature her so much she might even some day learn to make her bed before going to school.

My daughter has now reached the negotiating phase of her adolescent development and everything is a debate.

"Sweetheart, you need to clean up your room."

"It's not messy. It's just the way I like it."

"Clean it up or you can't go and play with your friends."

"Can my friends come over and help me clean?"

"No."

"How about if I clean up half my room and only go out and play with my friends for half the time I usually do?"

"No."

"How about I clean up some of my room and play with my friends for just some time?"

"No."

"Daddy, that's not fair."

"If you don't clean your room you'll stay inside and not see your friends until they're old enough to be grandparents."

"I'll try."

One of the first things we had to do was decide what pet we were going to get. Since I'm fully aware of my daughter's negotiating techniques I knew she would start large and I would have to start small. She began by wanting an elephant. I suggested a paramecium. She came down to a hippopotamus, I went up to plankton. We went back and forth for an entire weekend and finally decided on something called a gerbil.

Gerbils are lovely creatures that make wonderful first-time pets. They look like mice trying to imitate kangaroos. Their existence is centered around eating, sleeping, chewing stuff, jumping and digging. It's a simple existence but one they seem to enjoy.

Prior to its arrival we got all the things necessary for a gerbil. A cage, chewing sticks, gerbil food, a wheel, a water bottle, saw dust for the bottom of the cage and a cardboard box for the gerbil to run around in and chew into nothing. We all felt like we'd created a virtual gerbil nirvana.

The day we got the gerbil it was brought home and carefully put in the cage with all its gerbil stuff. We watched it run around, dig in the saw dust, sniff the water, jump around awhile and go into the cardboard box. I thought that was it and left my daughter alone to be with her new pet.

I soon learned that a child's perception of having a pet and a parent's perception are two different things. My child didn't want to just observe the gerbil, she wanted to interact with the gerbil. She wanted to be on the cutting edge of the gerbil little girl experience.

It seemed important to her that she open the top of the cage, stick her hand in and try to pet the gerbil. For his part the gerbil didn't take to this very well. I imagine if some creature twenty times my size took the roof off of my house and stuck their hand in to get me I might understand just how upset this poor creature must have felt.

He ran into the box, she took him out of the box, she tried to grab him and he jumped around and squeaked.

Squeaking is a gerbil's way of saying, "Hey I'm an observation type animal. If you want something to interact with get an elephant."

That's when we experienced our first pet catastrophe, the gerbil got loose. My daughter handled the great escape well. She watched him run around her room and yelled for her parents. My wife and I formed a gerbil posse and set out to catch the little critter that just jumped, squeaked and ran around my daughter's bedroom. We eventually herded him into my wife's hands and he was put back into his cage. The little gerbil continued to run around, sniff at things and jump over stuff. It appeared as if he had suffered no permanent debilitating, psychological gerbil trauma from his journey outside the cage.

We soon discovered that gerbils are nocturnal. That means he makes a lot of noise at night and makes it difficult to sleep. Because of this he was banished to the downstairs game room for all his nocturnal activity.

The gerbil was the center of my daughter's world, for about a week. After that time she discovered the gerbil wasn't like a toy. It had to be fed, given water and the cage had to be cleaned.

"It's time for you to clean your gerbil's cage."

"I don't want to."

"How would you like it if you were that poor gerbil and nobody wanted to clean your cage?"

"I'd just have somebody's parent do it."

"Just clean the cage."

By the end of the month the gerbil had evolved from something my daughter was with constantly into something my daughter began to regret.

"Dad, did you ever have a pet like this?"

"Yeah."

"Good, then you can take care of it because you know how."

"No, what I'm going to do is teach you how to take care of your pet. That's what we parents get to do for our kids."

"Teach them to do stuff they don't want to do?

"Exactly."

We all developed our roles in caring for the pet. I made sure we had plenty of gerbil food in our house and checked that his water supply was adequate. My wife endured our daughter's complaining and made her responsible for cleaning the cage and refilling the food and water. In a matter of time my daughter developed an ability to take care of things on her own.

The pet turned out to be a very valuable experience. The gerbil was able to show us how we worked together as individuals and let us see how we could work together as a team. It all came together for us as we all learned to care for someone new in our family.

HORSE SENSE

There usually comes a time when parents feel like they've experienced so many things and seen so many things that they know the outcome of events prior to them even occurring. This has always set me up to experience many of life's lessons like I'm a student unaware I'd even enrolled in the course.

It was a cool fall day when my daughter walked into our home after an exhilarating day of school and announced she wanted to take horse-riding lessons. I instantly responded in the most fiscally responsible manor possible. I explained that horse-riding lessons were expensive, dangerous and probably not something that we could afford to do for her.

My wife calmly listened to my speech and when it was done turned to my daughter and said, "We'll look into it."

After putting many miles on our car and watching many young girls ride horses we decided to give one place a try. It was within our budget and close to our home. I also learned that one of the other parents had previously read an article of mine and heaped much praise on me. This was obviously the best choice we could make.

Prior to this experience I pictured horse-riding lessons consisting of my daughter simply going to the stable, getting on a horse and riding it while someone instructed her. With my daughter I learned that in addition to riding instruction she had also developed her very own horse lesson protocol.

Upon arrival to the horse stable she had to go around to pet, greet and pull out a scrap of something from her pocket to feed every creature in sight. This of course is accompanied by talking to, petting, playing with all the creatures and maybe forgetting why we're even at the horse stable. The next step is to greet all her horse friends and attempt to put her parents in the poor house by providing all of them with carrots.

Finally comes the horse lesson but prior to even getting on the horse she must talk to the horse and tell the horse about her day. This assumes the animal anxiously waits to learn about the never-ending saga of her school decomposition project.

Once the riding lesson is complete she must then discuss such important issues as her favorite gum with the instructor. The final phase before leaving the stable is to find all the creatures she said hello to when arriving because they would all be crushed should she not hunt them down and say good bye to them as well.

Things were going pretty good and the instructor said my daughter was doing very well for her age and never having ridden a horse before. Then one day they informed us there would be a horse-riding competition at the school and wanted to know if we'd like to have our daughter participate.

My wife simply shrugged her shoulders and said, "why not?"

My daughter got excited and said how much she'd love to be in the competition. I got a knot in my stomach.

There were some children at that school who came from some very serious and dedicated horse riding families. Many of these children's parents could afford to buy them horses and pay to have the best of everything associated with horse riding. I'm ashamed to admit it but I felt intimidated. I didn't want my daughter to experience a crushing defeat at her age. I understand dealing with such things is a part of life and I resigned myself to accepting the fact that whatever the outcome this was something that had to happen.

Prior to the competition I tried to lecture my daughter on how winning wasn't everything and sometimes just knowing you gave it your best was its own best reward. My daughter responded to my worldly lectures with a shrug and a nod of agreement before going back to doing her homework.

On the day of the competition there were horse trailers everywhere as many children prepared for their turn to ride. Some of these children wore beautiful complete English riding outfits. My daughter wore what had been borrowed, given to us by families whose children had out grown it or loaned to us by the riding school.

Many of the other children and their parents were very focused on what was happening. Parents drilled their children and rehearsed in anticipation of their turn to compete. Prior to her ride my daughter was busy feeding barn creatures, talking to horses and probably had forgotten why she was there in the first place.

Right before it was my daughter's turn to ride I looked at her and tried to say something profound but what came out was for her to have fun and try to not step in any horse manure. Not the best words of wisdom but it was all I could think of to say.

Prior to even getting on the horse my daughter had to talk to the horse, pet it and I think she may have invited it to dinner one day the following week but I'm not sure.

During her ride the horse responded wonderfully and my daughter was all smiles and appeared to be having the time of her life.

When things were over all the riders went to the center of the riding arena so the winners could be announced. There were eleven children and after some of the bottom names were called the knot in my stomach began to unwind. When they got to the top of the list I was pretty sure my daughter might even get some type of a ribbon and that would be great.

When they announced my daughter as the winner my knees went weak and I let out a yell as if she'd won the World Series. The other children were very gracious and congratulated her. My wife cried and I was yelling, screaming and wanted to carry her out of the horse-riding arena on my shoulders.

After some pictures my daughter gave us her blue ribbon and headed down to the barn to inform all her barn creature friends and horses she had won.

I needed that experience. I'd forgotten all the things money can't do for a person. Money bought horses and the beautiful riding clothes but it couldn't buy the joy that comes with doing something for the love of it. Love that comes from inside and expresses itself in desire to be the best. The blue ribbon didn't mean as much to my daughter as the experience and doing what was special to her.

POLITICAL COMPROMISE

Politics is a powerful force that always exists in many ways throughout our lives. There are governmental politics, office politics, sports politics and best of all family politics.

In my home there are three distinct and different political factions each having their own unique and specific agendas. I'm the conservative with my platform consisting of freedom for all people to watch sports, pro fixing things with duct tape and equal access to deep dish pizza for all. My wife is more of a liberal with a platform that is strongly pro shopping, defending the rights of people to eat out and feels that talking for long amounts of time on the telephone is something protected by the Federal Communications Commission. My daughter is a strong independent. She believes watching videos is an inalienable right of all kids, she is pro playing computer games and supports the taking of stuffed animals everywhere she goes even if it's to school or church. With those well-defined political beliefs our family government can get more than a little interesting.

Recently an issue came before the floor of our house, which was our dinner that had fallen there. Since we were all tired and hungry I suggested that we go out to eat after we clean up the mess. A spirited debate to rival any in Washington D.C. occurred as we attempted to solve our dinner crisis.

"I want to go to Burger Playground!" my daughter yelled.

That earned a groan from my wife who offered her own solution to our dilemma.

"I'm not in the mood for burgers. I'd like to go to Le Expensive Restaurant to eat."

Neither of these ideas suited me and I felt I had in mind the perfect dining experience for us all.

"How about we go to the Greasy Cheapo Restaurant for one of their specials?"

For some reason this suggestion earned a groan in unison from both my wife and daughter. With our positions clearly stated we all began to debate on our house floor as we cleaned up our dirty kitchen. My daughter went first.

"Burger Playground is the best place to go because they give away toys, have a playground and paper place mats with games and puzzles on them."

My wife didn't buy this argument and shot down my daughter's idea.

"Oh, I couldn't handle that right now. Little kids running all over the place and parents yelling at children who are throwing food at each other. I'm tired and I want to go to Le Expensive Restaurant."

Now it was my daughter's turn to attack her mother's idea.

"Mom, that's a boring place to go eat. I can't see my food because they don't turn on the lights and only let you see with candles."

I decided to join ranks with my daughter and then see if I could win sympathy for my cause.

"We can't go eat at Le Expensive Restaurant because it'll cost more than our total food bill for three weeks."

My wife shrugged her shoulders.

"You're exaggerating. It'd be the total of two weeks food bill at the most. Why do you want to go to the Greasy Cheapo Restaurant?"

Now was the time to play my hand. I opened a drawer and pulled out a piece of paper and began waving it as if I were at a sporting event.

"Very simple. I've got a coupon."

I know my wife and daughter are close but even I was amazed at how those two simultaneously sighed, rolled their eyes and looked away. It was almost as if they were a part of some synchronized whining team. Now it was their turn to attack my idea as I valiantly attempted to get them to see things my way.

"Dad, the Greasy Cheapo Restaurant smells."

"That's not a smell. That's the aroma of wholesome American cuisine being prepared for its dedicated patrons."

"Mike, I'm not going there. A person's cholesterol level increases quite a bit if they just look at the menu. After you eat in that place you can almost feel your arteries clogging."

"Does the fact that I have a two for one, kids eat free coupon make a difference?"

Again in unison I heard "No."

They did this so well I wondered if they actually practiced this when I was at work.

The situation quickly went from bad to worse as tempers flared and emotions ran high. My wife threatened a strike, my daughter threatened to boycott taking baths and I was ready to fine them all for being in contempt of Dad.

In the end we did what any group of people who were hungry and tired of arguing would do, we reached a compromise. We picked a restaurant that had a little of something we all requested, but not everything we all wanted.

Compromise is a wonderful thing that's an important part of being in a family. When you're in a family it's not always important to have your own way. But it is important to always have lots of respect for each other's opinions.

UNTECHNO DAD

I got a call from my daughter the other night. We had a nice conversation but I told her the next time she wanted to talk to just walk from her bedroom into the living room where I'm sitting. She asked me what we were having for dinner and when I told her I didn't know, she said she'd just call her mom in the kitchen. I guess I should be grateful she's not going around our house yelling.

Sometimes it feels like the advances in technology are causing the world I've always known to slowly slip away while being replaced with a world where people only communicate through machines. There was a time I didn't feel it was asking too much for my family members to speak with me face-to-face when they wanted to talk, but now I'm not so sure. The other day I asked my wife if there was anything planned for the upcoming weekend and her answer made me wish for the good old days.

"Oh, you can read all about the weekend plans on our family website I created. All the information is on there and I was even able to download a few pictures. It just looks so nice. I can't wait until you see it."

I was beginning to lose my battle to remain calm.

"What? I don't want to go to a family website to read if we're going to dinner with the neighbors or visiting your annoying relatives. I want you to look at me and just tell me. Is that asking too much?"

For some reason my wife didn't detect my frustration and seemed a little upset with my assessment of her family members.

"My annoying relatives? Just wait until you see what I put on our website about your relatives. I have some pretty good pictures I can scan into our system."

"Can you just tell me what we're doing this weekend?" I pleaded.

My wife smirked and said, "I'll send it to you in an e-mail."

She then turned and quickly left the room. I felt like saying something rather negative about her motherboard but decided against it.

My daughter has no idea that there was a time before the Internet, e-mail, video games or cell phones. The mere thought of a life without such technology seems to scare her.

"Yes, sweetheart when I was your age I spent a lot to time with my friends making up games to play, going on bike hikes and building tree houses."

"Didn't you play computer games?"

"No, there were no computer games to play."

My daughter gasped and her eyes went wide as she seemed very shocked.

"Next thing you know, you'll tell me there was no e-mail or Internet."

"I'm afraid when I was growing up there were none of those things."

My daughter began shaking her head and quickly left the room muttering something about her father growing up in medieval times.

I was getting a bad attitude about all the new technology in my life. I was starting to resent how it was taking control of everything I experienced. Feeling overwhelmed I needed to hear a friendly voice. I decided to discuss my feelings with someone who has provided me with a lot of advise over the years whether I wanted it or not, my dad.

When I explained my frustration he looked at me and calmly shared his ideas on the subject.

"I know just what you're feeling. I thought things got out of hand when everybody got televisions in their home. People just didn't talk like they once did," he said.

"We just started talking about television programs," I replied.

"Then everybody had a telephone in their house and nobody visited like they did at one time."

"With some of our relatives that could be considered a good thing," I said.

My father stood up and said something about me taking after my mother's side of the family before he left to get some water. I began to realize that technological advancements have always brought us both good and bad things and there's no way to stop progress. When my dad returned I got a call on my cell phone.

"Who called you?"

"My wife."

"What did she want?"

"She sent me a text message just to let me know she loved me."

I guess it doesn't really matter how we communicate with each other at times as long as we're sure to communicate all the right things.

UNRECOGNIZABLE

I have a daughter who is now old enough to attend the middle school. There are many things that change between the time a child leaves elementary school and goes on to the next phase of their primary education. Our daughter's change this year has been amazing. It seems the new job of my wife and I at this point in our daughter's life is to be sure we don't let on like we are actually her parents. This new stealth-parenting role is very important and is to be obeyed in public places and especially around her friends. It appears only acceptable to acknowledge our existence when she's hungry, wants some money to go shopping, is sick, hurt, needs help with homework or has won at an extremely difficult computer game. These are now the only moments that we can properly be recognized as her parents.

"Like who was that who gave you money?"

"Ah, those people over there like gave it to me. It was that guy and lady who are totally waving to me. I really have no idea like who they are but if they don't stop it I'm going to seriously call my extremely wealthy, young, attractive and very cool parents and tell them to quit giving these people money to give to me."

Whenever her friends are around we are expected to melt into the surrounding area and behave as if we are chameleons. If we are needed we will be acknowledged at a place far away from where her friends are located. This is important because if any of her friends actually discovered she did have parents it would cause her social humiliation on a scale that we parents just couldn't comprehend.

I've spoken with some other parents and have discovered this behavior of "I'm too cool for parents" is not at all unusual for someone her age. A fellow father said his daughter asked if she could tell her friends she was just renting a room in their house. Another parent told me his child introduced him and his wife as their home's butler and maid. As much as they do for their children it was hard to argue.

It has been explained to me that the reason for this desire to eliminate the reality of parents is because a new set of strict social rules are being pressed upon our children at this time in their life. Peer pressure is at an all-time high and anything that can give an edge in social standing is considered. This may even require a child's parents to act as if they've turned into the amazing invisible couple.

I recently went to a sporting event at my daughter's school. My daughter was involved with the event being held. Before it started the girls were in a circle getting ready for the start of the competition. They were all very busy launching disapproving glances at any parent who got too close to where they were standing and threatened their cool status.

During the competition the cheers and waves of parents could not be acknowledged as a kid's social standing could be lowered almost instantly for responding to an encouraging parent. When the event was over the children preferred their parents just wait in the car for them. The reason for this was so the children could just get in the car and refer to their parents as that nice chauffeur couple that works for their real parents.

Some parents respond to this situation with a feeling of sadness or a feeling of being rejected. There are others who view this situation in a more positive way and feel this behavior is sort of a blessing. Gone are the days when punishment consisted of grounding the child or taking away television and computer privileges. The new and preferred method of behavior modification is now a threat to arrive at their school and wave to them as they sit in class. The only punishment worse than this is for their parents to visit their child's favorite mall hang-out wearing nothing but their bathing suits. It's an effective motivational tool and many parents now prefer using this "parental appearance" threat method for disciplining their children.

As I am told this phase doesn't last forever. When children reach their early twenties they're usually more than willing to not only acknowledge their parents existence but to ask for financial, material and other types of help on a regular basis. Parents happy once again to be recognized are usually more than willing to help.

I understand that at this time it's important to understand such behavior is all a part of the growing up process. It is the child trying to give an image of independence from their parents when the reality is that they're still very dependent.

It usually doesn't matter to parents because they know that like so many other things with a growing child this behavior will also pass. What's important to a parent is that their children know they'll always be there for them.

When a relationship breaks their heart, if they're confused or afraid of a situation or need some advice on what to do in their lives their parents will always be there for them. It's not a matter of children acknowledging mothers or fathers but a matter of children knowing in their hearts they have parents who will always be their parents no matter what happens.

A COMMITMENT IS A COMMITMENT

There are many things during your life as a child which are surrounded by a cloud of mystery and only become clear as you get older. Things such as why your parents always got upset about having to pay these things called "bills", why people always have a reaction to the three letters IRS and why all those trips to the dentist really were necessary.

My father brought my personal adolescent mystery to new levels when he would respond to my request to quit certain situations by informing me quitting was not an option.

When I'd complain he'd give me a stern look and say, "Because a commitment is a commitment."

It was a versatile phrase he used in a variety of situations as I grew up. I remember hearing this phrase one Sunday when my father went to the store and got newspapers for some elderly people who lived on our street. He'd routinely stop by to see them and would ask if they needed him to get something. He would always take the time to go and get whatever they wanted.

These people weren't our relatives and when I asked why he took his time to help them my father would just shrug his shoulders and say, "Because a commitment is a commitment."

When I told him I didn't understand he'd just look at me with a smirk and say "Oh you will, someday. Trust me. I know you will."

So much for clarifying the complexities of the world for me in a way I could understand.

As I got older my father would use this phrase in key situations. When I wanted to quit playing baseball one year my father wouldn't hear of it. I'd had a run in with the coach and I felt that by quitting I would hurt the coach. I knew I might hurt myself but I foolishly thought it would hurt the coach more.

My father wouldn't hear of it and when I protested he looked at me sternly and said "Because a commitment is a commitment and you don't quit what you start until it is finished."

I reluctantly made it past that baseball season. During that season I hated every practice, every game and every moment. After it was all over the coach and I came to an understanding and I was glad I stayed on the team. I even completed one more season before I found something else I wanted to do more than play baseball.

As I grew older I heard this phrase of my father's many times. It's what my father said to me the day that I told him I wanted to quit the military because it was too difficult. It's the phrase I heard from him when I said I wanted to quit college because I just couldn't do it. It's what I heard from my dad during holidays when I told him I didn't want to see any of our relatives who were visiting.

The power of that phrase became very evident to me because as it turns out I finished my time in the military and I'm proud of that accomplishment. I finished college and was so glad when I got my degree. I even found ways to make the best of my relative's visits during the holiday season.

I finally understood the power behind that phrase the day I got married. Before the ceremony my father came to see me. When I looked at him I used the phrase for the very first time.

With my hand on his shoulder I said, "I won't forget that a commitment is a commitment."

My dad smiled and said "That's a good idea but I just wanted to know if you've seen your aunts around here somewhere. They're supposed to be here by now."

After we laughed he looked at me and for the first time in my life I realized the phrase was now mine to use.

I've come to realize what my dad was trying to tell me. Life is full of commitments and how we handle them says something about us. Commitments to ourselves, those around us, our community, our family and our religion are important. It says something about the type of person we are and about the parents who gave so much to us.

The other day I was with my daughter when she was practicing her violin. She was getting frustrated at the progress she was making and told me she wanted to quit. I told her quitting was not an option.

When she protested I said, "Because a commitment is a commitment."

She looked at me with a confused expression and said "I don't understand what that means."

I looked at her and with a smirk on my face and said, "Oh you will, someday. Trust me. I know you will."

0-595-33580-2

Printed in the United States
24940LVS00005B/352-432

9 780595 335800